Reuen Thomas

Through Death to Life

Discourses on St. Paul's great resurrection chapter

Reuen Thomas

Through Death to Life
Discourses on St. Paul's great resurrection chapter

ISBN/EAN: 9783744755511

Printed in Europe, USA, Canada, Australia, Japan

Cover: Foto ©Thomas Meinert / pixelio.de

More available books at **www.hansebooks.com**

THROUGH DEATH TO LIFE

Discourses on

ST. PAUL'S GREAT RESURRECTION CHAPTER

BY

REUEN THOMAS, D.D.
Harvard Church, Brookline,
AUTHOR OF "DIVINE SOVEREIGNTY," "GRAFENBURG PEOPLE," ETC.

BOSTON
SILVER, BURDETT & COMPANY
6 HANCOCK AVENUE

———

LONDON
JAMES CLARKE & COMPANY
13 FLEET STREET
1891

Typography by J. S. Cushing & Co., Boston.

Presswork by Berwick & Smith, Boston.

TO THE MEMORY

OF MY DEAR FRIENDS,

THE REV. WILLIAM ROBERT PERCIVAL,

MRS. RICHARD JOLLY, MRS. WILLIAM KEYTE,

MR. JOHN FRASER AND MR. THOMAS MUSCUTT,

WHO, DURING THEIR TOO BRIEF RESIDENCE HERE ON EARTH,

MADE SO MANY HOURS OF MY LIFE DELIGHTFUL,

I DEDICATE THESE DISCOURSES.

"He (Emerson) believed in quotation, and borrowed from everybody and every book. Not in any stealthy or shamefaced way, but proudly, royally, as a king borrows from one of his attendants the coin that bears his own image and superscription." — O. W. HOLMES.

"The greatest is he who has been oftenest aided." — RUSKIN.

PREFACE.

THESE expository discourses have been publicly uttered from the pulpit in the regular course of my ministry. They are printed because so many persons who have been bereaved have expressed to me their deliberate judgment that they are likely to be helpful to a wider audience than that which listened to them. I have thought it undesirable to make detailed references to the literature of the subject, or to the learned men whom I have consulted in the preparation of these sermons. Quotation marks all over a page are a disfigurement. Paragraphs will be found which probably owe even their structure to others. But it is enough that the sermons are at least as much my own as Shakespeare's dramas are his. It may be as well to state that I have derived help in the direction of verifying exegesis from Bengel, Alford, Wordsworth, Bishop Ellicott, Dr. A. M. Fairbairn, Professor Godet, Dr. Gloag, Rev. H. Burton, Dr. Oswald Dykes, Rev. J. A. Best, Dr. S. Cox, Rev. W. J. Deane, Canon Westcott, Dr. George Matheson, the great old book, West on the Resurrection, Canon Farrar, Dr. E. H. Plumptre, F. D. Maurice, F. W. Robertson, Dr. D. R. Goodwin (in Smith's Dictionary of the Bible), Leo. H. Grindon, Dr. Hanna, Rev. E. H. Sears, and others. My great aim was to present and enforce what to me was manifestly Paul's teaching in the great Resurrection chapter. If, tried by modern standards, Paul is heretical, that is no business of mine. Of course, if I had been writing prelections for a class-room, the form would have been entirely different. All I have aimed at is to "give the sense" of St. Paul in a way suited to the necessities and competencies of a listening Christian assembly. R. T.

PREFACE TO SECOND EDITION.

THE testimonies I have received as to the practical usefulness of these expositions of St. Paul's teachings on the Resurrection have been so many and from persons of such varied experiences and opinions, that I am disposed to congratulate myself upon yielding to the judgments of friends who persuaded me to put them into print. A clergyman of ninety years of age writes me: "In my long life I have read variously on this great theme. Nothing has so illumined the evening of my life as this book of yours." An "agnostic" confesses to being agnostic no longer. Bereaved fathers and mothers have conveyed their thanks for new courage and hope. Into the hands of several "appointed to die" friends have put the book; and the testimony from dying lips as to its helpfulness has been sacredly delightful. While, if I were treating the theme *de novo*, I should be disposed to do it somewhat differently, yet it is so satisfactory to know that the book has had a mission to hearts that specially needed its truth, that I commend it once again in its original form to the benediction of Him who is "the Resurrection and the Life." R. T.

CONTENTS.

		PAGE
I.	HISTORICAL	2
II.	PERSONAL	29
III.	THE ONE GENERIC FACT	43
IV.	THE LIFE-BRINGER	59
V.	BAPTISM FOR THE DEAD	75
VI.	THE RESURRECTION BODY	91
VII.	EARTH TO EARTH	103
VIII.	THE GREAT TRANSITION	119
IX.	THE STING OF DEATH	134
X.	CERTAIN REWARD	147

I.
HISTORICAL.

"As thinkers, mankind have ever divided into two sects, — Materialists and Idealists; the first class founding on experience, the second on consciousness; the first class beginning to think from the data of the senses, the second class perceive that the senses are not final, and say, the senses give us representations of things, but what are the things themselves they cannot tell." — EMERSON.

"I have heard that wherever the name of man is spoken the doctrine of immortality is announced; it cleaves to his constitution." — EMERSON.

I.

HISTORICAL.

1 COR. xv. 1-9. — Now I make known to you brethren, the gospel which I preached unto you, which also ye received, wherein also ye stand, by which also ye are saved; I make known, I say, in what words I preached it unto you, if ye hold it fast, except ye believed in vain. For I delivered unto you first of all that which also I received, how that Christ died for our sins according to the Scriptures; and that he was buried; and that he hath been raised on the third day according to the Scriptures; and that he appeared to Cephas; then to the twelve, then he appeared to above five hundred brethren at once, of whom the greater part remain until now, but some are fallen asleep; then he appeared to James; then to all the apostles; and last of all, as unto one born out of due time, he appeared to me also.

THIS fifteenth chapter of the First Epistle to the Corinthians seems to me to be a kind of synopsis of the teachings of the Great Apostle of the Gentiles. So many of the greatest questions which can be asked are introduced, that if we were to follow its thoughts from end to end we should travel over ground as varied and interesting to us mentally as Switzerland would be to us physically. I have often wished to do that which I am about to attempt; viz. to investigate the teachings of the Apostle Paul as given in this chapter. We read it at funerals, but whether we understand it is doubtful. It appeals powerfully to our imagination — speaking as it does of death and resurrection, of victory over death, and of immortality. If we were to use the language of mere critics, we should be inclined to say that in this chapter St. Paul had put forth all his strength, that if we wish to meet him when he is at his best we must encounter him on this field. Here we have the reasoner, the thinker, the man of vision, the teacher. Here we have him face to face with heresy and heretics. At one time he has his feet on the ground of well-attested historical fact. At another time he is soaring, eagle-like, into the most brilliant splendor of the out-poured radiance of revelation.

The most thoughtful men in our churches of to-day must perceive that we are in danger of a merely emotional religiousness. We need not only Christians of good intentions and right feeling, but Christians who are intellectually instructed, who are too robust to be scared out of their faith by bold and thoughtless sceptics, however energetic and dogmatic they may be in their denials. A faith that is half doubt is necessarily a most sickly kind of faith. A ship that after every bit of a voyage has to be put into dock for repairs is ever in danger of sinking. And a faith that is not intellectual as well as emotional can hardly stand the tossings and tumblings of these storm-swept days in which we live.

In the confidence that a close critical study of what the Apostle Paul has taught us in this chapter will strengthen our faith, by illumining our understandings, and thus brightening our hope, I ask you to join with me in the prayer for the influences of the Holy Spirit of God to rest upon and enter our spirits, that we may receive with meekness that word of God which is able to save our souls.

First of all, let us try to get some correct idea of the condition of the people to whom St. Paul addresses this letter. They lived in Corinth, a city of Greece having a most remarkable situation. It was on a narrow neck of land between two converging bays. It had the names of "the bridge of the sea" and "the gate of the Peloponnesus." It held the key to that beautiful southern part of Greece which stretches out like a mulberry leaf into the blue Mediterranean.[1] Overlooking the city was a vast citadel of rock, rising to the height of two thousand feet above the sea-level. From this eminence one of the most impressive views in the world could be had. The mountains of the Morea, the snowy heights

---

[1] See Smith's Dictionary of the Bible.

of classical Parnassus, the Saronic Gulf with its islands, even the Acropolis of Athens, forty-five miles off, could be distinctly seen; and then to add tenderness and beauty to the grandeur and majesty of the mountain scenery, there was not only the ever-varying smile of the ever-varying sea, but a wide table-land with vine-clad terraces sloping to the glinting and glistening bays stretching to east and west. Beautiful for situation was Corinth!

To this city came people from all the surrounding region. Every kind of Jew and every kind of Gentile was found there. It was a place as distinguished for its mental activity as for its commercial enterprise, a place as distinguished for its wealth as for its licentiousness. Here a Christian church was founded by Paul himself. This church was afterwards visited by Silas and Timotheus, and here Paul made the acquaintance of Aquila and Priscilla. Here, also, the eloquent Apollos ministered. The church was also noted for the growth of party spirit; so varied a membership could not soon be brought into unity. But as out of evil good so often comes, so in this case. No letters are so varied and so practical, no epistles so fervent and eloquent, as these to the church at Corinth. From them the whole Christian world knows what the true ecclesiastical spirit is as it was illustrated in Paul.

It was not a spirit of faction and division, but the precise opposite. Moreover, the very heresies of the people gave the occasion for those parts of the epistle which are most profound in their teaching and most eloquent in their utterance. In opposition to the spirit of faction, Paul asserts the ground of ecclesiastical unity. In opposition to the Sadducean spirit of some of the members of the church, he proclaims the great doctrine of personal immortality, in continuing and unbroken consciousness, for all believers in Jesus. Such was the general state of that Corinthian church when Paul addressed to it this letter. It was a church divided into factions and disturbed by heresies.

How did Paul act toward it? Did he call a council and advise the expulsion of some of the members? Not at all. He had formerly insisted on the expulsion of a member who had married his own father's wife. That, said the Apostle, is intolerable. Hold no fellowship with that man. But on matters of heresy and faction he pursued an entirely different course. He did not demand the expulsion even of members who denied the doctrine of personal immortality. Strange as that may seem, it was a fact, — showing the large tolerance of the Apostle. But neither did he let them alone. He poured around them, as in this fifteenth chapter, such a flood of light that they must have perceived how entirely they had misapprehended the teachings of Christianity. He sought diligently to instruct them, and thus to convert them to the truth. If we are clearly to understand why the Apostle wrote as he did, — why thus and not otherwise, — it is necessary to acquaint ourselves with the views of the body and its relation to the soul held by the men of that day. That which men believed was coming to them with the Messiah was chiefly a regenerated condition of society; a new kingdom — a new order of things — prosperity and purity. Many persons came into the Christian Church with that hope. But more than this, these persons had certain views and opinions as to the cause of evil. They associated it with the material body. To be liberated from the body was everything. When any one spake of "resurrection of a body," they could not accept it, because in this flesh and blood, so they assumed, dwelt all the evil to which they were subject. And so they were in danger of what we may call an ultra-spiritualism, which ultra-spiritualism naturally runs into antinomianism and asceticism, with other evil conditions. This was their mental state; this was what the philosophy of their time taught them socially. They lived in that wealthy and licentious Corinth, — with its feuds and factions, arising out of the variety of people there; mentally they had been taught that all evil belonged to a flesh-and-blood body, and that to be disembodied was to be, in that act, liberated from sin and evil. And when St. Paul spoke to them of resurrection, they said: "Yes; whenever society is regenerated, there is a resurrection."

Now the Apostle saw clearly, as we must see, that it was necessary, once and for all, to grapple with these mental difficulties, because one error leads to another. If men do not believe in continued, personal existence in an embodied state, their ideas of a future life and of immortality become so shadowy as to mean nothing. Before we get through this chapter, we shall see exactly what the Apostle taught, and what he did not teach. We must patiently follow him step by step. It will be a good lesson for us, showing us that there is only one Christian way of dealing with "heretics,"— a hard and ugly word. All error is founded on some truth. Men who think are always liable to think wrongly, *i.e.* inadequately, but better that than no thinking at all.

No men are more unpromising, morally and intellectually, than they who are too lazy to do any thinking, who shelter themselves under the platitudes "that one thing is as good as another," and "that all views and opinions have something good in them"—that "providing you do as well as you can, you will come out all right." We have no warrant in the New Testament for treating even such frivolous people with the contempt they justly deserve. Man is here to search for truth, and to search till he finds it. When he has found it, his reward, mentally and spiritually, will be great. And he will enjoy it all the more that he has had to search for it. Our God is not a foolish father who endows his son with a fortune, and keeps him thus in guilty idleness, parent of every form of vice, all his days. He puts us upon searching for truth. Thus he trains and develops our minds into power and competency for the discovery of still higher and profounder truth. The only Christian way to deal with error and heresy is to present the truth.

> "Mild light and by degrees should be the plan
> To cure the dark and erring mind;
> But who would rush at a benighted man,
> And give him two black eyes for being blind?"

The fifteenth chapter of the First Epistle to the Corinthians is Paul's great sermon to heretics within the Corinthian church. He does not call for their expulsion, but for their instruction. So should it be always and ever.

How does he go about this business of instruction? First of all, he lays a firm foundation in historical and well-attested facts. The gospel he had preached to the Corinthians was not simply a philosophy, or a set of opinions, or a set of doctrines. It was foundationed on nothing short of facts so abundantly attested that they would pass for what they were in any court of law. The facts are summarized in these few words: "Christ died for our sins, according to the Scriptures; he was buried; he was raised again the third day." These are the simple historical facts. Then the Apostle proceeds to summon his witnesses. First, Cephas; then "the twelve"—one absent; then five hundred brethren in one great crowd; then James; then all the Apostles—no one absent; "and last of all, as unto one born out of due time, he appeared to me also."

Paul puts a case supported by evidence which would have been received in any court of law in the wide sweep of the Roman Empire.

This testimony of his is not given a long while after the event, but while most of those who could be put on the witness-stand and sworn were living. And in the church of Corinth there was no attempt to invalidate the evidence. On the other side they had no case. All they could say was that these witnesses were mistaken: they thought they saw Jesus in his resurrection body; but it was a vision only. The answer to which is, Find in all history a case of a dozen men all being in such a subjective state that they all saw the same vision, or dreamed the same dream, at the same time. If that is difficult, indeed impossible, find us an instance of five hundred men who at the same time were so exactly alike, mentally and affectionally, that they all dreamed the same dream or saw the same vision. The Society for Psychical Research never, I believe, receives the uncorroborated testimony of one person, that he saw "a ghost," or heard a noise in a haunted house. But if three separate persons are similarly affected as to their perceptions, they admit that there must have been some external object affecting them. If we had the testimony of Mary Magdalene only, or of Peter only, or of James only, or even of Paul, while their lives would compel us to believe that there was no moral doubt that each of them saw Jesus, and while the four together would give a case of the strongest possible probability, yet, at some time or other, each might have been in so exceptional an ecstatic state of mind that the subjective became as if it were objective; they mistook the vivid and picturesque dream for an actual outside personage. The case would break down when Paul was put on the stand, for he had never seen Jesus of Nazareth, and could not conceive what he was like. With Peter and James, seeing Christ singly and alone, the difficulty of proving the objectiveness of the vison would be much greater. But when the appearance is to eleven, and then to twelve, and afterwards to five hundred — no case is in existence of five hundred men ever dreaming the same dream at one time, or seeing the same vision at one time, — in each case there must have been the objective appearance. In a word, the historical fact of the Resurrection in human form of Jesus of Nazareth after his crucifixion had ample and convincing attestation. St. Paul will accept no other view of the case.

There is other evidence to be had that the Apostle Paul had been very laboriously careful in searching into all the facts about this Jesus of Nazareth, after he had his own vision on the way to Damascus. I think if it were wise and proper for me, here in this place, to carry you on a tour of critical investigation, that it would not be difficult to establish the strong probability that Paul had not only (during those three years in which he was in Arabia) laboriously compared the accounts of Jesus with the old Jewish prophecies about the Messiah, but that he had done more. There is enough of intimation scattered up and down the New Testament in the Apostle's movements and in his words, to lead us to infer that he personally examined the witnesses. In the Epistle to the Galatians, i. 18, St. Paul distinctly states that he went up to Jerusalem to find Peter, and abode with him fifteen days. Is it conceivable that those two men could be together fifteen days, and Paul not use the time in getting at the facts about the Resurrection from Peter, the first witness he calls?

There is also strong probability that he, during those fifteen days, got to know all that other Apostles had to tell of the Resurrection facts. To show further the thoroughness which characterized the investigations of this man of Tarsus, when he writes to these Corinthians, quoting historical evidence, and especially the very remarkable evidence that Jesus appeared on one occasion to as many as five hundred brethren, he uses language which suggests that he had verified that fact also, and knew the most of the five hundred, or how could he say of them, "of whom the greater part remain to this present, but some are fallen asleep"? As if he should say to these people in Corinth: "Examine for yourselves; I can give you the names of the men. I can tell you who of them are still living, and where they live, and who of them have passed away." Paul seems to know each of these brethren. He has been observing the life of each, and the death of each. He has been keeping hold of the chain of witnesses, and marking when any link was severed by the grave. After giving the experiences of others, he gives his own, and he puts it in the same category with the other evidences. It was of the same kind to him personally — an objective historical fact.

Now, why is it so important that we should recognize the emphasis which St. Paul puts on the historical character of the fact of the Resurrection? It is important because when once we get away from the *facts* of Christianity we are not like a ship at sea, with captain and crew and chart and compass, — the stars above, the deep below, — but "like a painted ship upon a painted ocean." In the early days of the Christian Church, and in our day, there have been men of the Sadducean order who have been very willing to accept what they call "essential Christianity." They like Christianity as a sentiment, as a feeling, as an ideal of life. So far, so good. But they doubt the historical facts and the supernatural miracles. The latter are myths; the former, the mere allegorical scaffolding which you can take down when once you have your Christian ideals and Christian sentiments and feelings afloat in society.

Doubtless you have met with men and women who assume intellectual superiority and much of poetical sensibility, but who seem to have no backbone of conviction to their religiousness. There is a great deal of that sort of temperament to be found. They tell you, "We have all that is essential in Christianity; we believe in the Fatherhood of God, we believe that we are all the offspring of God, we believe in a Divine Spirit influencing the spirit of man, and we believe in a real, though perhaps not in the vulgar popular sense, personal immortality. In all essentials we are Christian." In the Corinthian church there were people of that order, and yet it was with the purpose to prevent their doing the harm that they were certain to do that the Apostle wrote these words. All religiousness that does not gather round a great personal centre, occupying itself simply with an ideal that is abstract, and with sentiments and feelings, is unreliable. It lacks fixity. It lacks strength. It lacks courage. It is weak and vacillating. We see it in the Positivists and Agnostics of our own day as much as in the Sadducees of Corinth. Christianity as represented by the author of "Literature and Dogma" is not New Testament Christianity. It is not the Pauline Christianity. Paul's Christianity was something more than a collection of moral precepts and prohibitions, something more than Matthew Arnold's "kindness and pureness," "charity and chastity." In order to keep that which is ideal we must keep that which is historical. The ideal of Christianity is found in no one but the historical Christ. If we lose him, we lose it. "He is the brightness of the Father's glory, and the express image of his person," — he and none other. As one has eloquently phrased it, "By historical Christianity we mean not any abstract truths, but those truths as actually existing in the life of Jesus Christ; not merely the truth that God is our Father, but the belief that though "no man hath seen God at any time, yet the only begotten Son, who is in the bosom of the Father, he hath declared him;" not merely the truth of the Sonship of our humanity, but that there is One above all others who, in the highest and truest sense, is the only begotten Son of God; not merely that goodness and spiritual excellence is the righteousness which is acceptable in God's sight, but that these are not mere dreams and aspirations of our humanity, — that they are actual realities, and have truly existed here below in the life of One, the man Christ Jesus; not merely the abstract law of self-sacrifice, but the real Self-Sacrifice, — the one atoning Sacrifice which has redeemed the whole world." Now to this historical Christianity the Apostle bears the strongest testimony when he comes to these facts, that Jesus Christ (after his Resurrection) had been seen by Cephas, and the other Apostles, by five hundred brethren at once, and by himself.

The human heart needs something more than creeds, doctrines, aspirations, ideals; it needs a

Divine Person in whom it can believe, in whom it can rest, in whom it can hope. Creeds, doctrines, aspirations, ideals alone, are like those fairy folk we see floating about in some midsummer night's dream — unreal and insubstantial. It is when the flesh-and-blood Jesus Christ — the man of Nazareth, the man of Calvary — comes into our life, dies for our sins, that he may deliver us from them, and rises over death that he may be our Rescuer from Death, that we are satisfied. When he comes, we are at home with him. He seems one of us — what we are destined to be. Our hearts rest in him, and our lives are renewed by his presence.

II.

PERSONAL.

"The more faithfully we can represent to ourselves the life, outward and inward, of St. Paul, in all its fulness, the more unreasonable must appear the theory that Christianity had a mythical origin; and the stronger must be our ground for believing his testimony to the divine nature and miraculous history of our Redeemer."

CONYBEARE AND HOWSON'S *St. Paul.*

II.

PERSONAL.

1 Cor. xv. 9. — I am the least of the apostles, that am not meet to be called an apostle, because I persecuted the church of God.

We need to notice, as a separate theme, this introduction, by the Apostle, of himself and his own experience into this chapter. What does it mean — this self-depreciation — this using of so abject a term as that in the eighth verse about himself — a term much more abject (*ectroma*) in the Greek than it appears in the English? What does it mean? This self-depreciation and then this self-appreciation? Why does the Apostle introduce himself here so dejected — so elated? What has it to do with the narrative? Does it add to it? Does it strengthen it? Is it required? Is it necessary? When a writer like this, a man with so much delicacy of soul, says, "as to myself," you may be sure that there is something impressive to follow. It is as if he should say, Could anything but the truth borne in upon my soul with irresistible and overwhelming evidence have changed me from what I was to what I am? Then he contrasts himself with himself — Saul the persecutor of the Church of God with Paul the Apostle. He suggests to them to account for the change if they can in any other way than that the risen Christ appeared to him. And so, in himself and in the entirely new direction of his life, he is a proof of the Resurrection of Christ of no mean order. If the other Apostles have a right in this narrative, so has he. If their testimony was admissible, so was his. An apostle was a man who had seen the Lord. Paul had seen the Lord, or he was not an apostle. That he had seen him was evident, for he had been a recipient of the grace of God — of the strength of God — of the sustaining power of God — in labors that were abundant; so abundant as to give him the first rank as a laborer. What could have changed Saul the persecutor to Paul the seraphic missionary — the man who had been in deaths oft — the man who had been stoned — been shipwrecked — been beaten with rods — been in prisons and dungeons — what could have produced so great a change? Something must have done it; something adequate to account for the subjugation of this imperious nature — this fiery will — this man capable of such sublime consecration, who was total and entire in what he did — no half-heartedness about him; a man of learning, of scholarship, of great intellectual force, of all-consuming zeal, great in heart, great in intellect, great in executive power, a man capable of the sublimest consecration; what could have changed him from Saul who persecuted the Church of God, Saul who assisted at the murder of Stephen, to Paul who valued his life only because he could pour it out in the service of Jesus the Christ? He had not been reasoned into this; he had not been bribed into it, unless shipwreck, stoning, castigations, dungeons, deaths, are of the nature of bribes. There was everything to lose (so far as this world was concerned) and nothing to gain. Some cause must be found for this change. None of the other Apostles could give a reason. They were, for a while, doubters. No one outside the band of the Apostles could account for it. There is nothing to explain to us why and wherefore the persecutor of the Church became its sublimest and most seraphic apostle except that given by Paul himself. The risen Christ appeared to him and claimed him for his own. Thus the case of Paul, from its very uniqueness, becomes one of the most important links in this chain of evidence which encircles the great fact of the Resurrection of Jesus.

Moreover, it was impossible for the Apostle to be silent when witnesses were called, as he said before Agrippa, that at the time of his conversion Christ expressly signified to him that his very purpose in appearing to him was thereby to constitute him "a witness," able to testify to the world on the very ground of his having then seen the Lord. Silence on the question that he himself was an independent witness of equal value with the rest, he would have regarded as treasonous.

But then when he is giving his testimony, as he contemplates the truth rising ever into grander magnificence before his vision, he is seized with shame and self-contempt and he says, " I, — a mere abortion of a man, — I, the least of the Apostles, that am not meet to be called an apostle, because I persecuted the Church of God, to me this Christ of God appeared." The more he knows of Christ, the more he loathes that old self. He regards it with contempt and abhorrence. "That Jesus should show himself alive after his passion to the eleven and other believers, who had previously loved and followed him, and that they should receive the ennobling commission which authorized them to bear witness to their risen Lord, was one thing: they might boldly bear their testimony and feel no shame. But that a man who, at the time when Christ disclosed himself to him, was fanatically blaspheming his name and persecuting those beloved followers of his whose names he had just been reciting, that *he* should put himself forward by their side to assume this supremely honorable function of witnessing as an apostle of Christ to his Resurrection, and this, too, on the precise ground of a manifestation of himself made to rebuke and arrest that guilty career of his, *that* the writer might feel would strike some at least, as a piece of effrontery bespeaking a most strange unmindfulness of the complexion of his own previous life." But silence would be cowardice. And whatever there was in the nature of this Apostle Paul, cowardice there was none. Ever and always he stood to his convictions. As Saul, he was zealous and brave. As Paul, the same. Now, among the virtues which make manliness, courage ranks high. Indeed, it may be affirmed that there is no manliness without courage. To say the thing he felt about himself and about Christ demanded in Paul courage amounting to heroism. To say that when he persecuted Stephen the martyr, and the Church of God, he was most entirely wrong, and to affirm that this Christ had appeared to him, that Jesus was the Messiah predicted in the Scriptures, that he was God's Christ, — to say this always and everywhere, and take the consequences, demanded courage of the very first order. No braver man than Paul ever breathed the breath of life.

It is a mistake to suppose that modesty and self-depreciation indicate a lack of courage. It is proverbial that a bully is generally a coward. Modesty and self-depreciation may get the better of courage. Many a man has been much less than he ought to have been because of his self-depreciation, because he shrank from doing the thing which, at a particular time, he ought to have done. And that may become a habit. Thus a man's natural ability of usefulness may amount almost to a cypher through want of a little courage. It is as Rev. Sidney Smith has said: "A great deal of talent is lost in the world for want of a little courage. Every day sends to their graves a number of men who have remained in obscurity because their timidity has prevented them from making a first effort. The fact is, that to do anything in this world worth doing, we must not stand back shivering and thinking of the cold and danger, but jump in and scramble through as well as we can. It will not do to be perpetually calculating risks and adjusting nice chances; it did very well before the flood when a man could consult his friends upon an intended publication for one hundred and fifty years, and then live to see his success afterwards; but at present a man waits, and doubts, and consults his brother and his particular friends, till one fine day he finds he is seventy years of age, that he has lost so much time in consulting his first cousins and particular friends that he has no more time to follow their advice."

We may take the case of this Apostle and so use it that it shall be of great worth to us in the way of light and guidance.

What are we to do when a new conviction comes into our life — a conviction, it may be, which puts us into collision with our former self? Paul had thought that Christianity was a new heresy; that these men who followed Jesus of Nazareth were impostors; that the most odious form of persecution was all that they deserved. He was sincere and zealous in all this; but as he was on his way to Damascus, armed with the authority of the civil power, he met Christ Jesus. The Risen Lord appeared to Saul with the question, "Saul, Saul, why persecutest thou me?" No thunder out of a clear sky ever was so startling and unexpected as this vision, and this question. He had run up against a great fact, — that Jesus was alive. What was he to do with it?

Let us remember that nothing addressed to the mind, to the heart, to the reason, to the conscience, is irresistible in the sense that a man is compelled thenceforth to act upon it. There is always room for disobedience. That fact was recognized by Paul. When he appeared before King Agrippa he made distinct recognition of this liberty that remained to him in the words, "I was not disobedient to the heavenly vision." He had the liberty, the power, to be disobedient, but not the will. When the light came he followed it.

And of what nature was his following? Was it excited and impulsive? Did he go straight into the battle with error and sin? No; he went into three years of silence in Arabia. There, without doubt, he studied the Old Testament Scriptures afresh. And when he came forth from his retirement, he had found that these very Scriptures did speak of this very Christ. When once the fact of this Jesus being alive had been put beyond all possible doubt, then, in the light of that fact, he had to examine all his knowledge afresh. And that meant deliberation. It meant pause, retirement, solitude. And so he went into Arabia, — with the old prophets and teachers in his hand, and the Spirit of God as his tutor. Not till after that retirement was he ready to speak intelligently, and with his heart and conscience all saturated with the new views of God and his relation to men. I think that there is a needful suggestion here for ourselves in these modern days. Often and often, with great want of wisdom (so it seems to some of us), have men been set to public preaching to others immediately after, in some revival meeting, their emotions have been stirred and confession of Christ as their Lord been publicly made. And the more of badness there has been in the previous life, the more notorious the men have been, the more needful it has seemed by their advisers that their case should be made public. In the light of the retirement into Arabia of the great Apostle of the Gentiles, I am compelled to make confession of my belief that such sudden precipitancy of an untried man upon the public is all wrong. If any such men have gifts which can be utilized, let them, ere using those gifts, go into some Arabia for three years and get to know themselves. Unless a man's conviction is able to go into retirement for three years and grow, it is not of much account.

But, then, say some, think of the time that would be lost! Souls may be converted in that time. Good may be done. Was there ever a time when a great man like Paul was so much needed as in those early days of Christianity? Here was a man of the very highest order of endowment, a man of great natural gifts, a man of burning zeal, a man linguistically and philosophically educated, and yet he must go into the desert solitudes where no man was for three years. In the silence of continued meditation he must get acquainted with himself and with his God as revealed to him in Christ Jesus!

And still another thought. In all of us there

are struggling contradictory feelings and tendencies. This passage, in which the Apostle represents himself as an abortion of a man and not meet to be called an Apostle, and yet glories in his abundant labors, confessing the grace of Christ in him, is it not very much what we find in ourselves? There are people who appreciate themselves intellectually who are constantly depreciating themselves religiously. "I am not worthy to be a church member,— a Christian disciple." What pastor does not have to encounter that again and again *ad nauseam?* What preacher who does not at times, and sincerely say within himself: "I am only an abortion of a man, I am not worthy to be called a preacher." But as Paul had to be an Apostle, notwithstanding his self-depreciation, so you and I have to be that to which we are called, or deny the Christ of God as an all-sufficient Saviour. It would be an act of deliberate disobedience, if I, feeling my utter unworthiness to be a preacher of the Gospel, should yet refuse to do it when I am called, inasmuch as I believe, intellectually and heartily, that Jesus is God's Christ, and came to be man's Redeemer and Saviour. But is it not equally an act of deliberate disobedience on the part of some of you to refuse to confess Christ before men, simply because you feel that you are not worthy to do it? Ought St.

Paul's inward conviction of his own utter unworthiness to have kept him from being the Apostle that he was? And ought our inward feelings of unworthiness to keep us from confessing Christ before men? Most assuredly not. The same spirit that enlightened him can enlighten us. The same power that sustained him can sustain us. What presumption to affirm, even to suspect, that Christ is not able to keep us in the faith! What limiting of the power and goodness of the Son of God! What limiting of the grace of the spirit! The rebellion of the Israelites of old showed itself, how? "They limited the Holy One of Israel." They said, "Can God prepare a table in the wilderness?" In a word, Can He provide for us? And that is exactly what some of you are doing who don't confess Christ before men. You deliberately prefer the voice of your own timidity, of your own self-depreciation, of your own sense of unworthiness to Christ's call. What else is it, but deliberate continued disobedience? If ever there was, in this world, a man who might have justified himself in shrinking from his future, it was Paul. That which was before him was tremendous in dire possibilities. But he went into it and trusted God to care for him and keep him. And that is the only course open to us, — to go ahead, believing that God is ahead all the time. No private Christian, no minister, no apostle, can make progress or get satisfaction on any other principle, or in any other way.

Yea, I will tell you something else: the farther along Paul got, the more he knew experimentally of God's love and grace, the worse he felt — the more humiliated I mean — that he had ever been a persecutor of Christ's disciples. "Only think! think of it!" (I hear him say), "I actually persecuted this Christ, that Stephen with the angel face, those meek men and women who only wanted to be allowed to love and serve him on whom their heart was set!" He felt mean enough. And when he called himself no full-grown man, but only an *ectroma*, an abortion of a man, so long as he was in that state, he meant it.

The practical immediate outcome of this passage, so far as we are concerned, is simply this: Do not allow your sense of unworthiness to have more control over your action than the call of Christ. Do what you see ought to be done in the light of the fact that Jesus is God's Christ; able to care for you; able to sustain you; able to do more than you can ask or even think; able to keep you from falling, and to present you faultless before the presence of his glory with exceeding great joy.

III.
THE ONE GENERIC FACT.

"I trust I have not wasted breath;
    I think we are not wholly brain,
    Magnetic mockeries; not in vain,
Like Paul with beasts, I fought with death.

"Not only cunning casts in clay:
    Let science prove we are, and then
    What matters science unto men,
At least to me? I would not stay.

"Let him, the wiser man who springs
    Hereafter, up from childhood shape
    His action, like the greater ape,
But I was born to other things."

TENNYSON.

III.

THE ONE GENERIC FACT.

1 COR. xv. 12-19. — Now if Christ is preached that he hath been raised from the dead, how say some among you that there is no resurrection of the dead? But if there is no resurrection from the dead, neither hath Christ been raised: and if Christ hath not been raised, then is our preaching vain, your faith also is vain. Yea, and we are found false witnesses of God, because we witnessed of God that he raised up Christ: whom he raised not up, if so be that the dead are not raised. For if the dead are not raised, neither hath Christ been raised: and if Christ hath not been raised, your faith is vain; ye are yet in your sins. Then they also, which are fallen asleep in Christ, have perished. If in this life only we have hoped in Christ, we are of all men most pitiable.

ONE of the most learned of English critics writes thus of the historical truth of the Resurrection of our Lord : —

"The letters of St. Paul are amongst the earliest, if not actually the earliest, writings in the New Testament. Of these, one important group has been recognized as certainly genuine even by the most sceptical critics. No one doubts that the Epistles to the Corinthians, Galatians, and Romans were composed by St. Paul, and addressed to the churches whose names they bear. Nor is there much uncertainty as to the date at which they were written. The most extreme opinions fix them between A.D. 52-59; that is, under no circumstances more than thirty years after the Lord's death. There can then be no doubt as to the authority of their evidence as expressing the received opinions of Christians at this date, and there can be no doubt as to the opinion itself. In each of the Epistles the literal fact of the Resurrection is the implied or acknowledged groundwork of the Apostle's teaching. The very designation of God is 'He who raised up the Lord from the dead.' In this miracle lay the sum of the new revelation, — the sign of Christ's sonship. To believe this fact and confess it was the pledge of salvation. On many points there was a diversity of judgment among the Apostles, and a wider discrepancy of belief among their professed followers, but on this there is no trace of disagreement. Some, indeed, questioned the reality of our own resurrection, but they were met by arguments based on the Resurrection of Christ which they acknowledged. Whatever else was doubted, this one event was beyond dispute."

We cannot appreciate the Apostle's argument in this chapter, or feel its full force, except as we recognize that it is built on an undisputed fact, — that of the literal historical Resurrection of our Lord. That admitted, and demonstrated by evidence of the completest kind, then what? The foundation is laid; now for the building. There were, in the Corinthian Church, some who doubted not Christ's Resurrection but their own. Their minds had been so trained and schooled in the philosophies of their day that when Paul spake of the resurrection or the regeneration of men they immediately put a different meaning into the words from that which he intended, — a meaning similar to that which some of the men of our day intend when they talk of the elevation and regeneration of society. They mean, simply, the bringing men into a more intellectual condition, into a more amiable and charitable mood towards one another, — peace on earth, good-will towards men, that simply and solely. It cannot be denied that among the men of the past, whom we call "Stoics and Ascetics," there were illustrations of spiritual and unselfish men — men of whom Socrates was the type — men who lived for an ideal virtue and goodness. That cannot be denied. But no mere idealism, no mere philosophy, has ever done much for the elevation of the great masses of the people. No one can deny the excellency of much which Emerson has written. The mind of Emerson was saturated with the Christianity in which he had been born and nurtured. But even with this, if we had nothing to guide us except that which Emerson has left, ninety-nine out of every hundred people would remain untouched by any influence which could renew them. The subtler-minded literary people would read him, and be enlarged, but the many would remain altogether outside his influence. Now, in St. Paul's day, there was a tendency to separate religious sentiment from historical fact, — to reduce even Christianity to a philosophy. There is the same tendency now. It is illustrated in the works of the most scholarly writer of fiction this century has produced. No one can refuse to recognize the glorification of unselfishness in "George Eliot's" books. Everywhere the mystery of our existence is illumined and ennobled by the sufferers and cross-bearers. She has given us, too, a most exquisite poem on immortality, but she does not mean what Paul meant by that word, — personal immortality beyond the grave. "George Eliot's" books need only to have inserted into them the historical Christ and personal immortality, and immediately they become Christian. There is nothing nobler in spirit to be found anywhere than some of her characters. If they are as castles in the air, they are castles noble in architecture, beautiful in symmetry. They lack a foundation adequate to support and sustain them. That is all; but it is a defect of the gravest kind. Any religion which is simply a combination of sentiment and philosophical abstraction is unenduring.

It has no backbone to it. It is not sunlight poured out from the sun, but only aurora borealis. It needs permanent eternal facts to sustain it. No form of religion can last which has not underneath it these permanent historical facts. So felt Paul; and when he would save the Corinthian Church from becoming a school of philosophy, he laid the foundation of his great argument in a fact which could not be successfully refuted.

In the passage I have read as our text, it is necessary to observe how the Apostle assumes that, in this Jesus of Nazareth, there is the same humanity as in ourselves. He is not something different from ourselves, only something more. Our nature is in him, and so our destiny is in him. That which is true of him is true of us. As to the Resurrection, one case proves it. If Christ has been raised, there is a resurrection of the dead; if there be no resurrection of the dead, Christ has not been raised. I would have you observe very carefully this assumption of the Apostle: that the Christ nature and our nature is the same, and that what is true of him is true of ourselves. Everything in this great argument hangs on the fact that, in all but sin, Christ Jesus is our brother, according to the flesh and according to the spirit. Whatever will come to him will come to us. Wherever the head goes, the body has to go. The same life is in the body as in the head; the same blood in the brain as in the feet. Christ and his people are one; one in nature, therefore one in destiny.

But supposing this Jesus be not raised from the dead, supposing he has not opened the gateway into immortality, what then?

1. As to the Apostles, what? 2. As to the ordinary disciples, what? 3. As to those which are fallen asleep, what?

1. *As to the Apostles*, we are "false witnesses," —false, not simply mistaken; we are liars, the whole twelve of us; we have said again and again, "We saw him after his Resurrection"; he spoke to us; he gave us commission to go into all the world. Peter heard him say, "Lovest thou me?" Three times he heard him ask the question. Three times he got the answer, "Feed my sheep"; "Feed my lambs." I, Paul, heard him ask, "Why persecutest thou me?" And I said, "Who art thou, Lord?" and the answer came, "I am Jesus." We have attested solemnly to these things, Peter and myself, and the others. We have suffered, day in and day out, hunger and thirst, every form of persecution, risked our lives over and over again, for the pleasure of telling a lie which has landed us in poverty and disgrace. What do you take us for? Madmen, fools, liars. But we

are all that, if Christ be not raised. So spake the Apostle. He would not tolerate any compromise position. He did not strive to find a standing-ground between positive assertion and positive denial. Resolutely, and without wavering, he held on to the facts in all their simple and sublime literalness. How different this man's way of speaking from that which some religious teachers of our day adopt! They try hard to find some standing-place between positive assertion that Jesus was the Christ of God, and positive denial of his claims over men. They talk of his "moral influence"; what! the moral influence of an impostor? There cannot be a doubt that this Jesus claimed a place which no ordinary man can claim without blasphemy: "I and my Father are one." "Then they took up stones to stone him." They who took up stones knew what was involved in that claim. Supposing any teacher living were to use the language as to himself which Jesus used, what would his congregation do with him? Not stone him, exactly, but put him within stone walls. They would rightly deem that such a man was fit only for a lunatic asylum. Yet, knowing what Jesus did, we never accuse him of blasphemous egotism and lunatic conceit. It seems to us perfectly right that he should say of himself what he did say, and take the homage which Peter offered him, when he said, "Thou art the Christ, the Son of the living God."

And here, perhaps, is the place to remark upon a characteristic of apostolic preaching which we have not noticed sufficiently, viz., that it was not simply, or specially, the preaching of the Crucifixion of Jesus, but specially the preaching of Jesus and the Resurrection. The Crucifixion alone would have meant defeat; anyway, in the highest expression of it, the disgraceful martyrdom of a good man. Its influence could not have been more or other than that of Socrates, when he drank the hemlock. Add the Resurrection, and the whole aspect of things is changed. The life becomes not simply a martyrdom, but a revelation, a triumph. Man's mortality is thenceforth the mortality simply of that which is of the earth, earthy. The great fact is his immortality. Death itself is no longer a terminus, but a tunnelled gateway into life. How altogether different our thought and feeling would be to-day if this event of the Resurrection of Jesus had not taken place!

2. *As to the ordinary disciples, what?* if Jesus had not risen. Two consequences: their faith was an empty faith, and they were yet in their sins. Now what is an empty or void faith? Is it not a faith which has no centre, an empty thing like a soap-bubble, a filmy something floating in vacancy?

We should never divorce the idea of faith from an object. Talking of faith in the abstract does very little good. The question always comes up. "Faith in whom?" For faith must have a person to whom to cling. St. Paul says to these Corinthians, If Christ be not raised, what is your faith worth? Faith always assumes the one believing and the one in whom belief reposes. Is it not evident that faith towards God will be strong or weak, according to our conception of what God is? If the Eternal One sent Jesus Christ into this world, and then treated him so as the Crucifixion indicates, — filled him with unselfishness that was sublime, and then left him to be murdered by bigoted Jews, — what kind of a God is that to trust in? If there be no resurrection, the Crucifixion was not only a crime committed by the Jews, but — we dare to say it — it was a crime in that deific region, with which we do not associate crime. If the life of Jesus stops at Calvary, what does it say? Simply this: "I may be the best of men, spotless, sinless, with a consuming love in me for men, and yet get nothing for it but murder, — murder, foul and most unnatural!" How can one build up a religion on that foundation? How can one build up virtue on it? What an appalling mystery life would be if the Creator, whom we call Father, should evolve into being such a soul as that of Jesus, simply to dash it into nothingness! No doubt of this being a devil's world, if there be no Jesus the Christ now living in the joy of his glorified life. There is no person for faith to cling to if Jesus be not raised.

But that is not all. "If Christ be not raised, ye are yet in your sins." There has no one come to lift you out of them, no deliverer, no rescuer, no redeemer! The idea that Christ lifts us out of our sins, and separates us from them, is one of which we cannot make too much. The parent sin of all sins is this separation from God. We are children. If we are such children that we have no trust in, or love to our parents, what monsters we are! Or, what monsters our parents are, — one or the other! When you say, "I have no faith in that man," have you not said your worst? And when you say, "I have no faith in God," have you not said your worst? But, if he let Christ Jesus be murdered, you can have no faith in him. If that Christ came to live the life of perfect love, so that he might reveal God; if he came to say, "Now I have lifted you out of your sins, trust me and love me, and you will abundantly please God," then how can you help having faith in God? St. Paul says this is what he was, and this is what he came for. Is it not something for us to think about, that, apart from the personal Christ raised from the dead, our faith is vain and we are yet in our sins? Remembering, that on the Apostle's lips the word resurrection implies immortality, we may urge upon a sceptic such questions as these: "When you have taken away this belief in immortality, what single motive can be brought forward to liberate a man from selfishness? Will you tell him to live for posterity? What is posterity to him? Or for the human race in ages hereafter? But what is the human race to him, especially when its eternity is taken from it, and you have declared it to be only mortal? The sentence of the Apostle is plain: "Your faith is vain, ye are yet in your sins." Infidelity must be selfish; if to-morrow we die, then to-day let us eat and drink; it is but a matter of taste how we live. If man is to die the death of the swine, why may he not live the life of the swine? If there be no immortality, why am I to be the declarer and defender of injured rights? Why am I not to execute vengeance, knowing that if it be not executed now it never can be? Tell us why, when every passion is craving for gratification, a man is to deny himself the satisfaction, if he is no exalted thing, no heir of immortality, but only a mere sensitive worm endowed with the questionable good of the consciousness of his own misery?" These are the questions which infidelity has to answer.

3. *As to those who have fallen asleep, what?* "Then

they also which are fallen asleep in Christ are perished." Fallen asleep in Christ! What a suggestive word is this, — so full of rest and quietude! Not dead, only sleeping, and sleeping in the embrace of Christ. But those of whom we thus think are not in this beatific state. If Christ be not risen, they are perished. We cannot believe that. There is something in us which will not consent to that view of the case. There are some whom we have had on earth whom we really loved, who are gone hence. Their going was a loss to us; oh, how great! Relatives, friends, children — how dark the day on which they went! How lonesome the world became! The morning came, but they came not; the evening hour of quiet domestic life, but the chair remained vacant; the unoccupied room, the silent chamber, the unowned clothes, the very playthings that seemed widowed; the handwriting that came so often, yet never often enough from the postman's hand, — all these mute memorials! Where is he? she? it? my child, my friend, the one who loved me above all others, — where? Gone? Yes, but where? Into the silence and darkness, — a silence out of which speech shall never come, a darkness that has penetrated into my very soul! There is something in us that will not be satisfied with silence and darkness. Whence that something within? How came it? Why does it last? Why persist? Why will it not go out as a quenched light? Answer these questions, ye who are wise! Everything has a cause and a sufficient cause, — every thought, every feeling, every conviction, every intuition. The idea of immortality is in my mind. How did it get there? How could it get into a mind not preadapted to receive it? Then this intuition is corroborated by Jesus the Christ. "In my father's house are many mansions; if it were not so, I would have told you." As if he should say, "You have in you intuitions of immortality, trust them. They are right. Follow them; they will lead you to your father's house. What is this world? A world of beginnings, of seeds, of germs, of embryos, of promises that never get fulfilled. A world of mistakes and errors, and trying experiences; and yet, a world in which it seems that everything troublesome and wrong might be easily otherwise. But deep down in every nature there is this feeling, that some day and somewhere the idea that is highest must be realized, and the expectation that is universal of something better and more satisfying must be gratified. "Now see," says one, "what these sceptics require us to believe: that all those who have shed a sunshine upon earth, and whose affections were so pure and good that they seemed to tell you of eternity, perished utterly as the selfish and impure! You are required to believe that the pure and wise of this world have been wrong, and the selfish and sensual all right." But how can we believe it? The thing is impossible. The Resurrection of Jesus the Christ says that they who have fallen asleep are not perished; they are in his keeping to whom all power is given in heaven and on earth. Then he has the power to save them, and keep them; the will, also. Why should he not save them and keep them? Perished! Why, even the material does not perish; it changes, but that is all. Why should the mental? Why the spiritual? If matter is indestructible, that which is superior to it must be. The Resurrection of Jesus is the great Yea of God to all man's longings for immortality.

IV.

THE LIFE-BRINGER.

"What is so universal as Death must be benefit." — SCHILLE

"Oh, yet we trust that somehow good
    Will be the final goal of ill,
    To pangs of nature, sins of will,
Defects of doubt, and taints of blood;

"That nothing walks with aimless feet;
    That not one life shall be destroy'd,
    Or cast as rubbish to the void,
When God hath made the pile complete;

"That not a worm is cloven in vain;
    That not a moth with vain desire
    Is shrivel'd in a fruitless fire,
Or but subserves another's gain.

"Behold we know not anything;
    I can but trust that good shall fall
    At last — far off — at last, to all,
And every winter change to spring."

                                  TENNYSON

IV.

THE LIFE-BRINGER.

1 COR. xv. 20.—But now hath Christ been raised from the dead, the first-fruits of them that are asleep.

THE moment we read these words we become conscious of plunging into great deeps. The ocean of being is over our head, and underneath our feet; and we swim in it, dive in it, and try to explore it in vain.

Standing on the great historical fact, "now hath Christ been raised from the dead," the Apostle immediately begins the discussion of the meaning of it. Perhaps that word "discussion" is the wrong word. It ought to be the exposition of the meaning of it. But his exposition is of the nature of suggestion only. He regards Jesus the Christ as the first-fruits of them that are asleep. The word "first-fruits" points us back to the Jewish ordinance, that the first of all ripe fruits should be offered in God's house. Until this ceremony had been performed, no harvest work was to be done. It was a public acknowledgment of the fact that Almighty God was the author of fertility and the giver of abundance. No mere verbal acknowledgment, apart from the offering of the thing itself, was enough. And, says the Apostle in another place, if the first-fruits be holy, the lump also is holy. In this chapter he regards our Lord as the first-fruits of them that sleep. He is the beginning of that great Resurrection harvest, when those who have disappeared shall again appear. The offering of first-fruits stood for the whole harvest. And so, Christ Jesus, the first who appears as the Conqueror of Death, is the pledge that all who share his life shall so appear.

Then the Apostle goes on to recognize that as we are related to Adam, so also to Christ. Here we get into deep water. I can swim in it, but I cannot dive to the bottom. We can say this much: as Adam was the head of the race physically and psychically, so Christ is its head spiritually, and as to those immortal elements that are in us. Adam brings death to us. Christ brings life to us. We inherit the Adam nature, and so the tendency to sinfulness which is in it, the death which is in it. But we also have life brought to us and freely given to us in Christ. The one is set over against the other. From Adam we inherit the mortal part of us; from Christ the immortal. Death came to us through man; deliverance from death came to us through man also. St. Paul is speaking of what occurs within the limits of this human sphere. He is speaking of the conflict of the mortal and the immortal. He speaks of it in general and antithetical terms; but with a boldness and breadth which are startling. The passage, "As in Adam all die, so also in Christ shall all be made alive," is one of the most sweeping of antithetical affirmations. Again, I say, it goes beyond my ability of interpretation. I cannot see to the bottom of it. The "all" on one side of the antithesis must be measured by the "all" on the other side. It would be simple trifling with language to affirm that a paraphrase like this expresses all the meaning that is in it: "As in Adam all men die, so in Christ shall all Christians be made alive." That will not do. Alford says it refers to physical death, and rescue from physical death. If that were so it would read, so far as its meaning is concerned, "As in Adam all partake of physical death, so by Christ all are rescued from physical death." But what about the fact that we all have to partake of physical death? It is here in our midst, a universal and undeniable fact. Infants die, children die; in maturity of life, as well as in old age, men die. Every one of us must taste of death, or death must taste of us. I very much question whether the death that came to us in Adam was physical death at all. The narrative in Genesis does not seem to suggest it. St. Paul, so it would seem, is the wisest interpreter of the old Genesis record.

In expounding this passage I should prefer to say that the Apostle is intending to impress upon us, in a general and antithetical way, that all that was mortal came to us in Adam; all that was immortal came to us in Christ. If we had nothing but that which came to us in Adam, we should all die. But we have more. We have the Eternal Life that is brought to us in Christ. The Adam nature was but the ground in which the indestructible seed of the Christ nature was sown. Christ interprets Adam. The why and wherefore of Adam's existence is not found in Adam, but in Christ. I am convinced that we cannot understand St. Paul so long as we think of Adam as God's ideal man. He was not that.

Before we get through this chapter we shall discern this more clearly. What was Adam, then? He was the type of the man who has in him everything that is merely natural and psychical without that which is spiritual and Christian. I think St. Paul suggests that. But I would speak with all modesty and not dogmatically on this matter. Adam represented all dying men and all that could die in man. And I would rather put the antithesis in this way: So far as we are in

Adam we die; so far as we are in Christ we live. Adam is a word standing for death. Christ is the word that stands for life. If we have nothing in us but that which Adam represents, we necessarily die; only in virtue of that which Christ brings to us do we live. Whether the Apostle intends more than that I do not know, but I think he must intend that much by these words: "As in Adam all die, so in Christ shall all be made alive."

Having made this general statement, he goes on to remark upon the divine order for the regeneration and resurrection of man. Every man in his own order. Christ is the first-fruits. A raised Christ is the beginning of a new order, and a new harvest of souls. Following Christ are those who have been Christians here on earth, so I take it: "They that are Christ's." Throughout the New Testament I think you will find this same order. In the Gospel of St. Matthew and elsewhere you find an acknowledgment of Christ and his followers, and then those who are not his followers. Christ standing in his own order — like as the head of our body is of its own order — then you find Christians his disciples, his followers; then a third order of men. You find a Christ, a church, and a kingdom which is not a church. There is a distinct recognition of this threefoldness in the mind of the Apostle, — Christ, the first-fruits; then they who are Christ's; then the kingdom which is not a church. Now, the more I read the Bible, the more it seems to be clear to me that it is intended as a Book for the Church of God in this world of ours, and that they who find everything in it concerning the destiny of all kinds of men, in all the eternal future, clearly and fully explained, find something which is not there. Nay, it seems to me impossible that it could be there, unless all the revelation that God has to make could be put into a few years of our earthly life, and into minds like ours that can only expand to a very limited extent, and under the conditions of time and space. When I say that, do not understand me to affirm that there is nothing definite and clear. That would be an entire misinterpretation of my meaning. But take this chapter. There is much which is not definite, not clear; and yet where the horizon recedes, it becomes gloriously rich in sunset colors. You have seen sunsets which — in language so ornate, that the prince of orators would be struck dumb by it; in colors so gorgeous that no painter could paint them — told of a fine to-morrow. You looked, and looked, and looked, and then sighed a deep sigh, or brushed away a tear, and turned to go on your way. And some of these passages of Scripture are like that sunset. Interpret them in words or on the artist's palette, you cannot; but you feel their wondrous suggestiveness. Now, as the highest reach of language is language which is translucent, the language of the true poet which lets light through it, and suggests more than it says, so the highest order of thought is that which gives you suggestions of something larger than itself. To-day we sit at the feet of St. Paul, and confess that we cannot see as far as he saw, nor interpret adequately much which he wrote. Well, I for one am glad of it. When one stands on a hill and looks afar, to the extent of the carrying power of the eye, and then recognizes that there is much beyond, to which all that we have seen belongs and of which it is a part, then our hope and energy are aroused. We are far more satisfied than when we are shut into a valley out of which we cannot see. Only, even there a sky is above us; an infinity stretches beyond the power of imagination's wing. There are some passages of Scripture which suggest an infinite beyond, without describing it. Listen as I read but this one: "As in Adam all die, so also in Christ shall all be made alive But each in his own order — Christ the first-fruits — then, they that are Christ's at his coming. Then cometh the end, when he shall deliver up the kingdom to God, even the Father; when he shall have abolished all rule, and all authority and power; for he must reign till he hath put all his enemies under his feet — the last enemy that shall be abolished is death."

Immediately the language turns upon something that does not pertain to Christ and "they that are Christ's" it becomes stately and obscure. It is as if we gaze from the top of some Alpine height. Everything melts into everything else, and the whole into the horizon, making a picture of sublimity with very little of definiteness. So long as we are on the plain, with the houses round us, and the villagers at their work, so long everything is definite and clear. And so long as the New Testament occupies itself with Christ Jesus and his disciples, — their character and their work, — so long it is clear and crisp in its utterances, but no further. Let us remark upon that which is clear : —

First. Christ's ability to redeem and save and keep them that are his.

Secondly. His ability to abolish everything which is in enmity to them.

Thirdly. Their inability perfectly to understand the work of Christ till it is accomplished. These thoughts are clearly inwoven into the texture of this narrative. Firstly. "Christ's ability to redeem, and save, and keep them that are his." The words "they that are Christ's at his coming" suggest that all Christian disciples are redeemed and kept in safety till the end of this present dispensation of things. And this is the one thought as to the condition of the redeemed which the New Testament makes emphatic, — they are in Christ's keeping. And therefore well kept, well guarded, in bliss, in content; but their state is not perfected; their inward condition is not fully developed. Yet we need have no anxiety about them. They are in his keeping, to whom they specially belong.

Now such language is accordant with our deepest feeling as to safety. When you send a child away from home, your chief anxiety is as to the character of the people in whose charge that child is. You know that everything else is secondary. With a sublime reticence the Scripture says little of the unseen world. But it makes much of the fact that they who are there are in Christ's most holy keeping. Whatever is good enough for the Son of God's love ought surely to be good enough for the other children of the family. "At Christ's coming" — whatever that may mean — his disciples shall appear, and be seen in their happy, contented, glorified condition.

Secondly. Christ's ability to abolish everything

which is in enmity to them. That, also, is suggested. The time will come when this "strong Son of God," in the exercise of his "immortal love," will have abolished all rule, authority, and power that is in enmity to him and to the life of his people. He must reign till he hath put all his enemies under his feet. The last enemy that shall be destroyed is death. There are "certain hindrances that at present prevent the perfect operation of God in our souls. Evil in a thousand forms surrounds us. We are the victims of spiritual and moral evil, and till this is put down forever, the completeness of the individual cannot be; for we are bound up with the universe. Talk of the perfect happiness of any unit man while the race still mourns! Why, the evils of the race fall on him every day. Talk of the perfect bliss of any spirit while the spiritual kingdom is incomplete! The blessing of the individual parts can only come with the blessing of the whole." Hence the Apostle's language about the whole creation groaning and travailing together in pain until now, waiting for the adoption, to wit, the redemption, of our body.

But St. Paul anticipates the time when all that is in enmity to redeemed men shall be abolished. The idea is too great to be appreciated by us. *We* want poverty abolished, and mental misery, and pain; then we opine that we could get on well enough. But our nature is other than that we think it to be. If we want to know our profoundest selves, we must look at Christ. He is the interpreter to us of our own nature. But notwithstanding the mysteries which lie infolded in our nature, let us in hope and faith wait the working out of the purposes of that strong Son of God to whom all power is given in heaven and on earth. He can remove all hindrances and abolish all enemies, even that dark-visaged enemy whose frown darkens our life so often; "the last enemy that shall be destroyed is death."

But another thought suggested to us is the inability of Christians to understand the work of Christ till it is accomplished. The apostolic language is so general, yet so full of hope and confidence, yea, even certainty, that it forces this thought upon us. Telling us so much, why does St. Paul not tell us more? The answer is: There are certain revelations which belong to earth; there are certain others which are not of this present condition of things, and cannot be told us except in the form of suggestions. Is it not so everywhere? Childhood cannot grasp the great language and the complex experiences of manhood. "I have many things to say unto you, but ye cannot bear them now," are our

Lord's recorded words to his disciples. Everything has its time and place. I am prepared to find that on many things concerning which we have sometimes been proudly dogmatic, we shall, in the next stage of our existence, discover ourselves to have been entirely in the wrong. Not wrong on the relation of the disciple to the Saviour; not wrong on the fact that faith in him regenerates and saves; not wrong on the worth of his redemption; not wrong on the necessity of the Holy Spirit of God to the life of man; — not wrong on these, but on such a question as the relation of the Church of God to that great unredeemed world which has gone into the measureless realms beyond the line of death. What will God do with his redeemed Church when he gets it on the other side? How will he use it? What activities and employments will he give it? Such questions will come up, and we cannot bid them down. Our God is training us and qualifying us *for what?* What is all the discipline of this lower life *for?* It must have a meaning and a purpose outside the individual. "No man liveth unto himself, and *no man dieth unto himself.*" God Almighty will not endorse any of that narrow, mean individualism in which men and women are simply worshipping themselves, and using others to promote their own pleasure or profit. He has made this human family to be so inter-related that no part of it shall be content, and happy, and perfected while other parts of it are depraved and demoralized to the extent of being inhuman. God has more light and truth to break out from his Holy Word on the relation of men to one another and to their future. Never in this world can we fully understand the great mysteries of life. That knowledge remains for the future. But we can hold on to the Saviour, in the assurance that only in *that* is our wisdom and our comfort.

There is not room for doubt that the Apostle Paul regards all men as having as real a relation to Christ as to Adam. Whatever of spiritual life is in the world, anywhere in any part of it, is from Christ. Whatever sunlight is in the world is from the sun. "I am the Light of the World." The more I hold communion with the mind of Paul and of John, the more I revere the Christ of God. But I do not count myself competent to interpret all their great language. I am persuaded there is more in it than I have got out of it. Words on a great man's lips mean almost infinitely more than they do on the lips of a small man. The only way to get the ability of a more adequate interpretation of Scripture is to become ourselves larger-hearted men. I cannot tell you how to do that except by becoming more

Christ-like in feeling and aim, and doing larger and nobler deeds in his name. But I am always struck with the great hopefulness of this Apostle. That the man who wrote those appalling words on human depravity, in the first chapter of the Epistle to the Romans, should cherish still the magnificent belief he had in the future of man, is remarkable. It must have come from his perception of the weakness of sin compared with the strength and glory of redemption. No man can read these verses from the twentieth to the twenty-eighth of this fifteenth chapter of first Epistle to Corinthians and fail to feel how vital they are — how hopeful — how victory and triumph seem to hide away in this great language. And it is all associated with the condensed truth in this one passage, "As in Adam all die, so in Christ shall all be made alive." Everything else seems to grow out of that. By the Christ, the Church and the Kingdom are to be interpreted. It would seem that Christ's Church has to do business in Christ's kingdom — that those who here on earth have been of his Church will have a rank not belonging to others; but the others, if not won by the Divine Love, are yet subjugated, brought under the divine order; when, how, I do not know; but the end is that God is all in all. There is the consummation "that God may be all in all." What a grand thought! What a magnificent hope! Whatever it may mean, this is the far-off divine event to which the whole creation moves, — "that God may be all in all."

V.

BAPTISM FOR THE DEAD.

"All rose to do the task He set to each,
 Who shaped us to His ends, and not our own."

SHELLEY.

"O Lord, that I could waste my life for others,
 With no ends of my own;
 That I could pour myself into my brothers,
 And live for them alone."   FABER.

V.

BAPTISM FOR THE DEAD.

1 Cor. xv. 29-34. — Else what shall they do which are baptized for the dead? If the dead are not raised at all, why then are they baptized for them? Why do we also stand in jeopardy every hour? I protest by that glorying in you, brethren, which I have in Christ Jesus our Lord, I die daily. If after the manner of men I fought with beasts at Ephesus, what doth it profit me? If the dead are not raised, let us eat and drink, for to-morrow we die. Be not deceived: Evil company doth corrupt good manners. Awake up righteously, and sin not; for some have no knowledge of God: I speak this to move you to shame.

THIS passage would seem to be in its wrong place. It ought, one thinks, to come after verse 19, inasmuch as it is the same kind of reasoning which is found in that and the preceding verses. It contains an appeal to certain facts which are meaningless and absurd, unless there is a resurrection life for men. The facts are these: baptism for the dead, a life in jeopardy in every hour of it, such violent contention at Ephesus that to the Apostle it was like "fighting with beasts," — these and such like facts, what meaning is there in them? how absurd they are! how unaccountable! how altogether foolish if the dead rise not into a new and higher life! The most unintelligible part of this passage is that which is contained in these words: "Else what shall they do which are baptized for the dead? If the dead are not raised at all, why then are they baptized for them?" About the meaning of this passage there has been much debate. There are no fewer than seven modes of interpretation. I should be needlessly occupying your time if I submitted to your attention the whole seven. Several of them are too ingenious to be probable. Only two of the seven, it seems to me, are of sufficient worth to be seriously entertained. The most learned expositors are divided between these two meanings. The first is that known as "vicarious baptism," the practice of believers in the Corinthian church of submitting to baptism as substitutes on behalf of believing friends who had died without baptism. There are traces of such a practice in early Christianity, though it was regarded as a superstition by the more educated and intelligent of men.[1] Tertullian alludes to it when he says, "They adopted this practice (of being baptized in room of the dead) with such a presumption as made them suppose that the vicarious baptism would be beneficial to the flesh of another in anticipation of the resurrection." Chrysostom, in a curious pas-

---

[1] See Exegetical Studies by Dr. Gloag.

sage, informs us that after a catechumen "was dead, they hid a living man under the bed of the deceased; then coming to the dead man, they spoke to him, and asked him whether he would receive baptism, and he making no answer, the other replied in his stead, and so they baptized the living for the dead."

Another ancient writer (Epiphanius) informs us that "among the heretics in Asia and Galatia, there was a practice when any of them died without baptism, to baptize others in their name, lest in the resurrection state they should suffer punishment as unbaptized."

It has been said that, though this was a mere superstition, yet without approving the custom, the Apostle quotes the fact, and simply asks, Why this custom of yours, if there be no resurrection state beyond the grave? If there be no resurrection, why do you allow yourselves to be baptized as substitutes for the dead? It is admitted that such a custom did exist among heretical sects. It is also admitted that the language used would bear, without any straining or violence, this meaning.

But would the Apostle Paul be likely to refer to such a superstition without condemning it? Would he use it as of any worth in the way of proof? If the baptism for the sake of the dead was itself erroneous, what is in itself false cannot be adduced as an argument in favor of a truth. One would suppose that St. Paul, with his veracious temperament, could not have referred to such a custom without anger. Even if it were well meant, and only a silly superstition belonging to ignorant people who were troubled about their friends having died without baptism, yet there was no fact at the back of it to give it worth. Quotation by the Apostle, without rebuke, would seem even of the nature of toleration, if not endorsement. And so we infer that this interpretation, endorsed as it is by men of great learning, can hardly be accepted as the true one, unless indeed there be nothing to supply a better interpretation.

The interpretation to which my own mind inclines as the true one is of another kind. In those times of persecution, when it was as much as a man's life was worth to be an avowed Christian, it was very remarkable how vacancies made by death of those who had been baptized were speedily filled by new converts stepping forward and taking their places. These, accepting Christian baptism, were regarded as baptized "for the dead." The ranks were often thinned, but as speedily supplied with new recruits. Persecution seems to have appealed to the hearts of the best, and to have stirred their courage into life. Men were killed; new men came and took their places. Is it not probable that to these the reference is? Because the Apostle is speaking of "standing in jeopardy every hour." He is speaking of turbulent times, of afflictive dispensations, of fighting with beasts at Ephesus, — men, that is, who acted like wild beasts. All this lends probability to the position that when he refers to baptism for the dead, he refers to the wonderful immediacy with which converts came forward and took the place of those who had been murdered for Christ's sake. Why do this, if there be no resurrection state? — no state beyond death? — no uprising from the tomb? How senseless, how absurd, how recklessly fanatical to act so, if there be no resurrection state! Why should anybody be so utterly foolish as to do it?

If this be the true interpretation of the Apostle's meaning, it suggests to us that the Christians of his time, notwithstanding all the heresies and errors which would naturally get possession of minds beginning to think on great themes, were a robust, manly, heroic race of men. What a touching scene it must have been to see the baptized rushing into the ranks of those who had fallen, nobly enduring the same sufferings, meeting the same doom! — like soldiers occupying the breach which death had made in their ranks, thus verifying the observation of Tertullian that "the blood of the martyrs was the seed of the Church."

In the presence of such a fact, ought we not to be stimulated to inquire how far we are worthy to be in the succession of such men and women as these who were baptized for the dead? This chapter brings us face to face with an age of persecution and heroism. The Apostle Paul stood for the character of the Christian disciples of his age. It was an age of violence, of turbulence, of dreadful foreboding. No man's life was safe. Every hour men stood in jeopardy. Dark uncertainty hung over everything. The clouds above were stormy; the earth beneath was treacherous. To any individual Christian to-morrow might be the day of death. The Christian assembly of to-day might never meet again in the totality of its brotherhood. At the next meeting half its members might have been seized, imprisoned, or confined in dungeons whose darkness was fetid with leprosy or some other dire plague. In those days tyranny gave no account of itself to justice; yet no persecution was dire enough or dreadful enough to scare many of the Christians into a denial of their Lord. It is a wonderful story. They must have felt that there was something in Christianity of priceless value. The dangerous times do not seem to have been those when persecution's hand was heavy. Then men clung to Christ and to one another. But when persecution's hand was relaxed, and times were placid and comparatively easy, philosophers began to speculate and to interpret in a manner not according to fact. Then the Epistles had to be written, lest the disciples should be drawn away from their simple faith in Christ. But notice how good came out of evil. These Epistles have been storehouses of truth from generation to generation. That which is spoken evaporates; that which is written remains. And so we ought never to be afraid of controversy as such. While we deprecate the method and spirit in which controversy is conducted, yet that is not owing to the matters in controversy, — only to the temper of the men who engage in it, — revealing oftentimes that it is not the supremacy of truth they are seeking, but only their own supremacy. A man should never enter into controversy until he has prepared himself for it. And how? What kind of preparation does he need? He needs just the kind of preparation which comes to a man's soul when, in prayer and supplication, he abases himself before God. Then he will seek to be entirely fair with his adversary, be, above all things, anxious to discover the truth, and in no other way to win a victory. There is great danger lest we should conduct controversies as gamblers play cards, or dicers handle dice. Then controversy, even about the truth, demoralizes. St. Paul was a great controversialist; but what thoroughness, what self-repression, what nobility, he everywhere showed! He refused to overcome evil with evil — he overcame it with good. How are you and I to show the erroneousness of any position which is erroneous? How does a housekeeper convince her help of the unclean and disorderly condition of a darkened room? Simply by letting in the light. That is exactly St. Paul's method in controversy. When the question of the resurrection life beyond death is in debate, he pours such a flood of light into the minds of the debaters that the question is settled, not for the Corinthian church alone, but for all churches. About the resurrection of dead bodies there may be debate for centuries; but there has been none worth speaking of as to the resurrection of the dead since Paul wrote to the Corinthians.

In the Church of Christ, as elsewhere, controversy is inevitable. Speaking generally, in the denomination in which there is most thinking there will be most controversy.

If, however, we strive to maintain the unity of the spirit in the bond of peace, all will tend to good. Timid souls deprecate controversy. They prefer stagnant to running water. Observing men note that only running water is pure. "The murmuring brooks that make the meadows green," fertilize the fields. Everything in creation has energy and movement in it. No generation has ever lived in which this fact is recognized so generally and so intelligently as in our own. Not a universe "of dead matter, but a universe everywhere alive" is the dominant idea of our day. And so, if we are every now and again stirred up by some controversy, let us take it as a sign that the Spirit of God is "moving on the face of the waters," that God himself is forcing upon us inquiries which we must make, in order that our life may be richer, ampler, and fuller. Let us not be angry with men who make us think; they are our friends. Our enemies are those who try to chloroform our minds — who administer a subtle opiate to our spiritual sensibilities, that we may dream instead of act. The man who gives me a new thought enriches me. The man who puts iron into my blood puts health into my blood. The man who in this world of snow and sleet keeps me moving saves my life. If the movement be an onward and an upward movement, every step is so much nearer to the Kingdom of Heaven. Every living man has something else to do than to vindicate the men of the past; he has to vitalize the men of the present. We cannot live in two generations at once. It is hard to live in one. Only that which is eternal is independent of time. Eternal truth belongs to every generation, and to the men of all time, because it is God's truth, the truth about him who is "the same yesterday, to-day, and forever." Nothing lives from one generation into another, unless it has in it the eternal truth of God. That is why the Bible lives and will not die; not because it tells us of Adam, or of Noah, or of Abraham, or of Moses, of Job, and Isaiah; not even because it tells us of Paul, and John, and Peter; but because it shows us God in union with man, draws aside the veil from the face of deity, and shows us "God manifest in the flesh." It is this eternal life, the life behind and beyond the temporal life, which lends such an awful fascination to these records. It matters not who is the speaker; if God speak through him, man must listen.

After this Apostle has appealed to the facts, of which they knew, in proof of the resurrection life, he comes down to that condition which is inevitable with men who do not accredit the resurrection state beyond death. "If the dead are not raised, let us eat and drink, for to-morrow we die." That is the inevitable morality of atheism, the seeking satisfaction solely in the gratification of the senses. Constituted as man is, he will fight no battle simply from sentiment or feeling. He must believe that there is something worth fighting for. In every one of us, the flesh lusteth against the spirit, and the spirit against the flesh, and these are contrary, the one to the other. This world was intended to be a battle-ground. "I came not to send peace, but a sword." Depressing and discouraging words unless there be something beyond! Everything on earth is lent us. Nothing really becomes ours till we have done battle for it. The earth and the heavens are full of knowledge, but we have to learn it. The only way in which we can make it our own is to struggle with it. Like Jacob of old, when he met the angel and had to wrestle for the blessing, so it is with ourselves. Everything external has to become internal. The fact without has to become the thought and feeling within before it is ours. Before this earth could be what it is, it had to be melted by fire, drenched by rains, swathed in fogs impenetrable by light. All this agony had to be endured. Before that bright spring morning which wakes up every bird, and excites every fragrance, and unfolds every leaf, could come or be possible, all that scorching fire, and drenching rain, and impenetrable fog had to be. Before you and your friends could meet around the parlor fire, and enjoy each other's society, the Creator had to make the coal whose red warmth casts its glow on your visage. *Create* it? What does that word mean? How much? Begin at the beginning and trace the geologic formation of our common coal from the time it was vapor till through endless ages it became forest, died into its unvitalized condition, and became hard as stone; then you will know what the word "create" means. If it takes so long to make the coal which is the concentrated energy of ages, is it a marvellous thing that it should take years and years — how many we know not — to form the soul of man into a capability of communion with all that is deific and godlike?[1] *A soul!* Who knows what it means? The atheist says "man grew." All these lower things conspired "to grow him." Wonderful things they must be! To-morrow we die; what then? Let us enjoy our senses, our passions. That creed means all and everything of devilism. It cannot support morality. It cannot support order and good government. It has nothing to say to a broken heart. It has no human word in it, much less a divine word. A dog has a better creed than that; he does believe in some one above him — in his master. He has attachment, affection, patience, faithfulness, endurance. Between an atheist and a dog, I prefer the dog, for his master is his God. "Blackfriars Bobby" that died on his master's grave in Edinburgh seemed to have a mute belief that his master lived still, and would some day call him.

---

[1] See Logic and Life, by Rev. H. S. Holland, M.A.

There is no well-bred dog whose life has not more in it than this wretched creed : let us eat and drink, for to-morrow we die. Yet there are those who assume that society would be as orderly and as pleasant to live in if we regarded our fellow-men as soulless animals, born into this world simply to eat and drink and die. The Apostle regards such as deceivers and deceived. He warns Christians against consorting with them, on the ground that "evil company doth corrupt good manners." No man standing alone, with the universe around him, and the thought of God writ in his own nature, would ever feel, or think, or act the atheist. But men in companies will pour their worst thoughts into each other's souls; each will add fuel to the fire that is in the other, till feelings, thoughts, morals, manners, are corrupted. Now, if this be true of men, if the influence on them of evil company is so debasing, what must it be on children? Yet, how careless are some fathers and mothers as to the company their children keep! We need to say to these, using the Apostle's language, "Awake to righteousness, and sin not, for some have not the knowledge of God. I speak this to your shame." Righteousness involves right discriminations; it involves a reasonable amount of asceticism; it involves carefulness in the associations of life; it involves (at any rate until the individual is strong enough to do missionary work in that direction) no fellowship with infidels and atheists. If a man has an atheistic tongue, I have no call to supply him with a pair of atheistic ears. It seems to me that the Apostle suggests that it is a shameful thing for a man to have no knowledge of God. There are three sources of such knowledge open to us.

1. The creation is one: "the heavens declare the glory of God, and the firmament showeth his handiwork."

2. Our own natures: the material is not all, mind and spirit are undeniable, and so the Creator must be mind and spirit.

3. The Revelation in Christ is a third source, and the highest, but it would amount to nothing if it were not adapted to our receptivity.

No man can entertain a thought which his mind was not pre-adapted to entertain. Do what you will, you cannot get the thought of God into the mind of an animal. Do what you will, you cannot keep it out of the mind of man. Man's nature was pre-adapted to it. But we may have the thought of God, and not the right thought. We may have thoughts of God without any correct knowledge of God. And yet "this is Life Eternal, to know thee, the only true God, and Jesus Christ, whom thou hast sent."

VI.
THE RESURRECTION BODY.

"The mould of each mortal type is broken at the grave; and never, never, though you look through all the faces on earth, shall the exact form you mourn ever meet your eyes again!" — Mrs. H. B. Stowe.

"The seed determines what the plant shall be, but it does not contain the plant." — Westcott.

"Could a mysterious foresight unveil to us this resurrection form of the friends with whom we daily walk, compassed about with mortal infirmity, we should follow them with faith and reverence through all the disguises of human faults and weaknesses, waiting for the manifestation of the sons of God." — Mrs. H. B. Stowe.

VI.

THE RESURRECTION BODY.

1 COR. xv. 35.—But some man will say, How are the dead raised, and with what manner of body do they come?

THIS great chapter seems to divide itself at this verse. The Apostle has been, up to this thirty-fifth verse, occupied with the Resurrection of the Christ. He has been showing that historically no event could be more abundantly attested. He has been connecting the life of Christ with the life of man, as the first-fruits are connected with the harvest. He has suggested that with the Resurrection of Jesus, a new dispensation of things was inaugurated. The Divine Triumph over Evil was first illustrated in the triumph of Christ over death: that was the promise, yea, the assurance, that Christ should reign till he had put all enemies under his feet, and the great Divine Order which was contemplated in the making of man could be established as the final order in creation. But this great and glorious result can be brought about only by the general diffusion of the knowledge of God, as that knowledge is incarnated in Jesus the Christ.

Beginning with this thirty-fifth verse, the Apostle Paul grapples with another part of the theme. The question, "How are the dead raised, and with what manner of body do they come?" is one that we have all asked. We see our relatives and friends die. We stand by the fatally sick one, and by and by the breathing ceases — the pulse beats no more — the features become rigid — the eye is glazed — the face looks as we have never seen it look before. There is no expression there. Soon the whole frame becomes cold, icy, rigid. And whether we are willing or not, we have to bury our dead out of our sight.

Something has gone out of that body. That which vitalized it has gone. That which we could not touch, nor weigh, nor measure has gone. That which made that body animate, interesting, and beautiful has gone. And of all dead things nothing looks so dead as a dead human body. Moreover, that which gave form to the body has gone; that which distinguished it from all other animate bodies. No sooner has this something, we might say this everything, gone, than the body immediately begins to disintegrate. It immediately begins to return to its dust.

Nothing can arrest it. We may embalm it, and hermetically seal it up — make a mummy of it; but a mummy is not a body. In the British Museum are many specimens of mummies brought from Assyria and Egypt, forms buried there thousands of years ago. They excite no human interest, only appeal to curiosity and create aversion. Let it be acknowledged that wonderful is this structure of the human body! If with the coldness of anatomists we could stand off from this organism and study its parts, we should be compelled to admit that there is no machine like it. But our business here is not with anatomy. Anatomy is at the best concerned with structure; we are occupied with that which necessitates the existence of these wonderful structures we call "bodies."

The necessity for this material body of ours arises from the fact that we belong, temporarily at least, to a material world. Without such bodies we could not see, or feel, or touch, or recognize this world. It would not exist for us. For a time we have to be bound to it — tied to it — confined within its conditions. Why and wherefore, we do not know; we only know the fact. It is the cradle of our humanity.

As we trace the history of man, we recognize how slow has been the growth of spiritualized intelligence, of mind power. Men have so identified themselves with this world as to make it everything. The Old Testament life was a life within earth-bound conditions. Only the very highest order of mind in Judea — in Egypt — in Assyria — in Greece — in Rome — rose to the conception of a life not bounded by material conditions. The religion of these peoples recognized that in order to have any blessing here on earth, and in order to be preserved from evils which might come upon them, it was necessary to propitiate and to seek the protection of the gods who made the earth. Their religion had relation almost exclusively to the present. Very few people rose to the elevation of thought found in that passage in the Book of Job, "I know that my Redeemer liveth, and that he shall stand in the latter day over my dust; and though worms destroy this body, yet without my flesh shall I see God."

It is only in Christian times, and among the most intelligent men of these times, that the human mind has risen to the perception of the fact that man can dispense with his material body and be the better for the deliverance. More than any other man who has ever lived, St. Paul has freed the mind from its slavery to material conditions. And if we follow carefully his thought as it is spread out to our gaze in this chapter, we shall get into our mind ideas which will lift us above the materialism with which not only pagan and heathen peoples, but also many only partially enlightened Christian people, still are burdened.

Not to anticipate the development of the Apostle's

thought in this chapter, let us recall what he says in other parts of his letters about this present material body. Writing to Roman Christians, he calls it a "body of death." He regards himself as tied to a dead body. He speaks of a redeemed body. To the Corinthians he speaks of it as a wild beast to be kept in subjection. To the Philippians he uses a most significant and expressive phrase, "Who shall change *this body of our humiliation* that it may be fashioned like unto his glorious body?" And, indeed, when you come to think what this material body is, and of what it is capable, how constantly it needs to be defecated and cleansed — how readily it contracts diseases, some of them of a most loathsome kind — how through it disease may be propagated, and how, as in the case of leprosy, it seems to become a disease in itself! — when you think of these things, you will not wonder that St. Paul should call it "this body of our humiliation." And yet, when we have said all this, to its disadvantage, we cannot withhold a recognition of the wonderful way in which the body, material though it be, sympathizes with and serves the purpose of the mind and spirit. The old Greeks, of all peoples who have ever been on earth, studied bodily form. They recognized its lines of beauty in their Dianas and Apollos. To a much larger extent than any other people, they lived for the body, — lived intelligently and artistically for the body; as it were, mentalized the body. But while they became the most artistic people the world has ever had, they also became thoroughly corrupt. They proved to the world, for all time to come, that the service of the body, of that which is external, even when artistically pursued, issues in enfeeblement, effeminacy and corruption. Art refines to a degree, but only to a degree. They who talk of regenerating men by opening art museums and multiplying picture galleries must be people with but little reflection. In Athens of yesterday, and in Paris of to-day, we have the most salacious of all populations. That true refinement which implies modesty, and the most delicate respect for womanhood, was not found in the ancient, nor is it in the modern city. When, however, we study the body under the influence of the mind and spirit, how admirable it often is — almost translucent, — at one and the same time revealing and concealing the thought of the mind, — the feeling of the soul! How often the very body seems to become mental, even spiritual, under the sway of strong, high, pure feeling, suggesting to us how possible it is to elevate even this body, and treat it as if it were a temple, — a temple of the Holy Spirit of God.

This body is a body of humiliation, and yet it suggests a body of a very much higher and nobler kind.

But notice this: as the mind develops and strengthens, as the heart enlarges and expands, as the nature widens and deepens, this body becomes steadily, and more and more unadapted to it. Age is not of the mind and heart; it is of the body only. The more tyrannous the body has been, — the more pampered and lived for, — the older does the man seem, as the years creep on. Spiritually-minded men, unless they have been slaves to mental work, do not become in feeling and spirit old, like men of the world. They often wonder at their own feebleness, because the spirit is just as willing as ever it was, though the flesh be weak. There is nothing that preserves juvenility like true piety. There is nothing ages men and women like the opposites of the graces of the spirit. Envy, hatred, jealousy, uncharitableness, — these bring the wrinkles into the face, and the age into the soul. Soul and body are so intimately associated that whatever brings hope, and faith, and love into the soul tends towards health in the body. I will make a present of that much to those of you who believe in mind cure.

But the body that is, is only the forerunner of the body that shall be. That much the Apostle states quite clearly. All the way through this chapter he is fighting the thought that we ourselves put into the phrase "disembodied spirits." St. Paul knew quite well that such an idea was inconceivable to a human mind. Everything limited must have embodiment. And so these people of Corinth, assuming that there was no body but a material body, and the material body being left behind, they had great difficulty in believing in the continued personal existence of those who were no longer occupants of that particular body.

Are there not many Christian people who have held some such view? How does the Apostle instruct these perplexed ones? He goes to nature, God's great parable, and finds a suggestion there. Only a suggestion — something looking in the right direction and pointing to the truth. Why, even in nature, he says, in your ordinary processes of sowing and reaping, you sow not the body that shall be, only a bare grain. The grain you sow remains in the earth, but the vital element that rises above the earth takes to itself a body suited to it. Every vital thing has in it a tendency to gather to itself a bodily form suited to its necessities and conditions. The grub in its grub state is embodied in one form and way; by and by, as it advances in its life, that body is no longer suited to it, but a new body is developing: soon it seems to die into its chrysalis state; but, lo, an entirely new creature, no longer with the limitations of the grub body, emerges; a creature that now sports in the air, and no longer crawls on the earth. It has its own body, but how different from the grub body; yet there is a vital connection between the one and the other. The life has been a continuing life. Each stage in it has been preparing for the next. Each animal thing has a body of its own, suited to its conditions. The seed has its, the fish its, the bird its, man his. All flesh, even, is not the same flesh. The fish could do nothing clothed in the flesh of the bird; the bird could not fly if he had the flesh of beasts. Everything has its own body suited to its state and its environment. That is the general thought to be first grasped. And not sameness, but variety, is the order of creation. There are terrestrial bodies — bodies that belong to earth. There are celestial bodies — bodies that belong to the heavens. And each and all of these have their special glory and beauty. A star is of one order, a sun of another, but each has its own glory. And so with bodies. There are some that are corruptible, others that are incorruptible. There is a body that belongs to man in his state of dishonor. Another which belongs to him in his state of glory. There is a body which is corruptible. There is a body which is incorruptible. There is a body which belongs to a man in his state of weakness; there is a body which belongs to him in his state of power. In a word, there is a natural body, and there is a spiritual body.

That is the climax of the Apostle's reasoning. The natural body is the type and promise of the spiritual body, but it is not the spiritual body. It has a relation to it, — yes. The same relation as the terrestrial has to the celestial; the same relation as corruption has to incorruption; the same relation as dishonor has to glory; the same relation that weakness has to power; the same relation that the physical has to the mental and spiritual. Everything lower points to a higher. Identity does not consist in retaining the same material elements, but in retaining that which is of the spirit. Through all the stages of his life, man remains the same — the same, yet different. Man is shedding his material body very gradually, and all but imperceptibly all the time, so that in ten years, not a particle of the old material body is left; yet he remains the same man. And, says the Apostle, man is never disembodied; all through time he is an embodied spirit, and when he has sloughed off his time body, his earth body, this body of his humiliation, he has still a body, but one suited to him in a way and to a degree to which this body never has been suited. There is the earthy body and the heavenly body. "And as we have borne the image of the earthy, we shall also bear the image of the heavenly." All earth forces and powers and laws have been in our earth body. Like the earth, it has been subject to the law of gravitation. Like the earth, it has been subject to decay; like the earth, it has been in constant change. We have borne the image of the earthy. "We shall also bear the image of the heavenly." The one is the promise of the other. The one is not complete without the other. The spirit of man in its next stage of being will have a body suited to it. Not a body subject to all the diseases, infirmities, neuralgias, aches, and pains to which this is subject. Not a body which cold can chill and heat inflame. Not a body which can experience hunger and thirst. Not a body which can be a tyrant or a slave. No; we have had this sort of a body. "We have borne the image of the earthy." The Adam body — we have had that. The Christ body — we shall have that. The beautiful human form will remain very much more beautiful than even in its Apollo strength and ideal loveliness it has ever been. Every one shall have his own body, the body suited to express his inward character; but it shall be as superior to this present material body, as the body of the butterfly is to that of the grub. "As we have borne the image of the earthy, we shall also bear the image of the heavenly."

VII.

EARTH TO EARTH.

"If there is a loathsome subject on earth, it is the subject of the human body." — ROBERT ELSMERE.

"In the whole history of human thought there are no grosser instances of slipshod reasonings and patent fallacies than those by which the so-called 'exact thinkers' have sought to rid us of our souls." — PROF. MOMERIE.

VII.

EARTH TO EARTH.

1 COR. xv. 50. — Now this I say, brethren, that flesh and blood cannot inherit the kingdom of God; neither doth corruption inherit incorruption.

ONE would suppose that it was quite impossible to make a mistake as to the interpretation of this passage. Its terms are so concrete, its affirmation is so clear and direct, that all simile, metaphor, figure, seem to be effectually excluded. And yet this passage has almost been overlooked by timid and nervous interpreters when they have been discoursing on the resurrection of the body. The word "body" has been interpreted so materialistically that difficulties have been created of the most serious kind. The resurrection of the dead has been interpreted to mean the resurrection of dead bodies. The word "body" has been interpreted to mean "material body." The direct teaching of St. Paul has been so determinedly ignored or so persistently and ingeniously explained away as to excite wonder at the audacity of interpretation in those who assume to accept the teachings of Christ and his Apostles as authoritative and final.

Men have compelled Paul to say what he manifestly never intended to affirm. On the contrary, that which he is teaching us, with such lucid and splendid reasoning, in this chapter is that there is a natural body and there is a spiritual body, and the one is not the other; nor can it ever be converted into the other. You will have observed, if you have followed St. Paul's development of thought in this remarkable chapter, that he begins with Christ's Resurrection. He does not interpret the mysteries of that great fact. As the sacred writer tells us, "Neither did his flesh see corruption." There was a period between the Resurrection of our Lord, the bringing him back to the earth-life, and the Ascension, in which he seemed, as to his body, to occupy an intermediate condition; a half-glorified condition. His body was not grossly material like our bodies are now. Some great change had passed upon it which made it almost independent of the laws of gravitation. He appeared among his disciples when the doors were shut. No barriers could impede or confine him. And yet mortal eyes could see that body. Through it speech could come into audibleness. That state seemed necessary to the full and perfect attestation of the fact of his Resurrection from the dead and his triumph over sin and death. But the forty days ended, and all the evidence of his Resurrection was supplied — all the evidence that the most rigorous necessity could demand. Then, while they beheld, he was taken up, and "a cloud received him out of their sight." The question has forced itself upon many minds: In that great transition from the visibilities of earth, to the invisibilities of heaven, did any change pass upon that body? In the light of St. Paul's teaching in the verses following this I have quoted as our text, one would incline to the belief that that partially glorified body of our Lord became wholly glorified ere the right hand of the Eternal throne was reached. That, however, is not fully and explicitly taught us. It is only an inference from what is taught. In the first part of this chapter the Apostle is occupied with giving the evidence of our Lord's Resurrection; his Resurrection in his proper human personality. Having done that, he proceeds to link the destiny of the disciple of Christ with that of our Lord. Then he begins to grapple with the difficulty which is contained in the question: "How are the dead raised, and with what body do they come?" Materialists cannot conceive of a body that is not materialistic. And a very large number of even intelligent Christians are materialists even now, and seem to be incapable of rising above that level. Clergymen often teach their people what St. Paul never taught his people. They teach their people that flesh and blood not only can inherit the kingdom of God, but that the subjects of that kingdom are in a most woe-begone and imperfect condition, until they get their flesh and blood back again. Nay, further: I know not whether there are any clergymen left who teach it, but I have heard of laymen teaching in Sunday-school that consciousness goes to sleep with the sleep of the material body — that soul and spirit are so inseparately associated with the material body that when that material body is buried, soul and spirit are buried with it, and remain asleep in the grave till God, by his mighty power, shall raise that body again.

It is marvellous that any one is to be found capable of believing even stranger things than the *bona fide* materialist believes. He believes that there is no life apart from an organism, and no organism but a material organism. You ask him what gives that material organism, its shape, and form? What makes it think and feel and hope and aspire and love? He cannot supply you with anything approaching to an adequate answer. The man who assumes that soul and spirit go down into the grave with the last of the bodies we have worn, necessarily associates all thinking and feeling with the possession of a material form and makes the material greater than the psychical and spiritual.

I venture to affirm that it is quite impossible, with

out prejudice and with perfect candor, to "mark, learn, and inwardly digest" what Paul has taught us on the resurrection of the body, and still believe that he means by "body" the flesh-and-blood body. This passage we use as our text is so simple and so direct that there is no controverting it. But lest some one should think there is room for hesitation as to his meaning, let us turn to his second letter to the church at Corinth. He speaks there of the perishing and decaying of the outward man, the flesh-and-blood body. He seems to recognize how great a trial it must be to a man, and especially to a woman, to find this outward organism, which is so attractive when the freshness of youth is in it and on it, decaying and becoming seemingly less and less effective for the purposes of life. They who have had much of satisfaction, and perhaps much of compliment, in possessing Apollo-like or Diana-like bodies must feel somewhat disconsolate when they recognize that strength and beauty are passing from them, and they are becoming very ordinary people. You young people who have attractions of person should remember that they cannot last, and never rely upon these external things for your happiness. Attractions of mind and character, those amiabilities and competencies which are of the heart and mind, last; they never fade. In those directions seek your development, and you will never have the disappointments which come to those who have to recognize fading beauty and waning strength.

But how does the Apostle Paul administer consolation to men who recognize that decay and infirmity have entered into the body? Listen. It bears very vitally on our interpretation of the theme we are considering. He is speaking of the bodily frame: —

"For we know that if the earthly house of our tabernacle (this bodily frame) be dissolved, we have a building from God, a house not made with hands, eternal, in the heavens. For verily in this we groan, longing to be clothed upon with our habitation which is from heaven; if so be, that, being clothed, we shall not be found naked. For we that are in this tabernacle do groan, being burdened — not for that we would be unclothed (disembodied), but clothed upon — that what is mortal may be swallowed up of life." How is it possible to take this language, add it to the language of this chapter, and then affirm that St. Paul ever taught anything like that which has been often taught, that the very particles of that material body which has been consigned to its earth are to be revivified and reconstructed in order to form a resurrection body? Of such gross materialism the Apostle Paul was incapable.

Of course the trouble is with this word "body."

St. Paul does not mean by it flesh and blood, and he most assuredly has no idea similar to ours when we talk of "disembodied spirits." If you had asked St. Paul, "Do you believe in the resurrection of the body?" he would have said, "Most assuredly." If you had asked him, "Do you believe in the resurrection of those dead bodies which we put into the grave?" he would have replied with emphasis, "Flesh and blood cannot inherit the Kingdom of God, neither doth corruption inherit incorruption." It is certainly true that so long as man is materialized in mind, he cannot conceive of any body but a material one. There are conditions in which it may not be wise to disturb the idea of a material body as the only body; like as there are conditions in which it is neither wise nor kind to turn a man out of a very tumble-down old cottage. Unless you can supply him with something better, leave him in his primitive ignorance and with his unwindowed raggedness. Even the dungeon of Chillon's Castle had become home-like to the long-immured prisoner. But in cases where there is intelligence and some degree of spiritual discernment, where faith totters under the load of difficulties it has to carry, then we have to go to the word and to the testimony. Then we have to put the most advanced apostolic teaching before the human mind, because it is ready for it, and demands it in order to the strengthening and the increase of faith. Nothing can be more indisputable to those of us who accept apostolic teaching as given under special inspiration of God than that the Apostle taught a bodily resurrection and denied a flesh-and-blood resurrection. Now if we affirm a flesh-and-blood body to be essential to our completeness as redeemed and regenerated men and women, we affirm what Paul denied. Moreover, we load our creed with most unnecessary difficulties; we materialize our faith. Death, instead of being the vestibule to a higher life, an advance on this, becomes a pain, a penalty, a disability. St. Paul says, "Knowing that while we are at home in the body we are absent from the Lord, we are willing rather to be absent from the body and to be at home with the Lord." Now, if we could get rid of our materialism and the remnants of our inherited heathenism, we could go to the grave with a lovelier as well as a livelier faith, and instead of burying our hearts in it, we could put our feet upon it, and knowing whereof we affirm, say, "he is not here, he is risen." That Christianity which does not help us when most we need help is of a very suspicious character and quality. It would be a heart-breaking thing to go to the grave and deposit there anything which was vital, anything which was necessary to the happiness or perfection of any one we really loved. Those scenes which in cemeteries and graveyards I have sometimes witnessed, when friends could not be torn away from the decaying material which was there deposited, are very sorrowful scenes. While they speak of a love which is impressive and beautiful, they also speak of an ignorance which is painful, and of a low spirituality which is depressing. And yet I suppose I should be counted a heathen, if on such an occasion I should say, "My good sir, or madam, there is nothing there in that grave but temporary consolidations of a little atmosphere, with a few pounds of phosphate of lime." Yet that is the literal truth of the case. If it were scattered to the four winds, it would make no difference to the happiness or progress of your beloved one. "But" — but what? "It was all I had left of my father, my mother, my child." Alas! alas! that any of us should be so unimpressed by the teachings of our Lord and his Apostles that we should ever feel like that! Outside of what remains there, *all* is left. And where there has been the true, vital thing we call "love," that love of God, whence it came, is sure to restore that which love needs for its perfecting. For that God, who is love, will never deny to love that which it needs for the completeness of its own life. That does not imply that all lives which have been tied together shall be retied. Nothing of that. But when our Lord said, concerning the sinning woman, "Her sins which are many are all forgiven, for she loved much," he let a world of light into the mystery of God's dealing with his creatures.

In the light of what he has taught us we can say that that which love needs for its perfecting God's love is sure to give. There is a Christian way of going to the grave. And there is a way most sorrowfully unchristian. And if by expounding this chapter I can get any of your hearts out of graves in which they are buried, and get them on God's good guardianship over spirits which, let loose from the bondage of the material body, fly into him as their home, I shall have helped you to a higher and more beautiful faith; a faith of such a quality, that though the tears must flow by the grave side, yet they are like drops of rain with the sun shining through them; that is the faith which becomes a Christian. But while we associate our departed with the graves in which their worn-out material shell is deposited, we cannot rise to that quality of faith.

Now, if we had studied St. Paul with open mind and intelligent appreciation, he would have delivered us from two mistakes, both of which are fatal to happiness and confidence in respect to the dead:

the one, that of trying to get a conception of "a disembodied spirit"; the other, that of believing in the necessity of the resurrection of the flesh-and-blood body which is returned to its parent earth. That foolish jesting about "ghosts" — using the word in a way to suggest unbelief and unreality — ought not to be encouraged, and especially in the presence of the young. The unreal thing on this earth is not spirit, but matter. It has no independent existence. Do you believe in spirits? asks one. Do I believe that there are persons without material bodies? Most assuredly. Thomas Carlyle describes old Dr. Samuel Johnson as anxious to see a ghost. He then remarks, Foolish Doctor! Did he never, with the mind's eye, as well as with the body's, look around him into that full tide of human life he so loved? did he never so much as look into himself? The good Doctor was a ghost, as actual and authentic as heart could wish; well-nigh a million of ghosts were travelling the streets by his side. What else was he? What else are we? It is no metaphor — it is a simple scientific fact. To think of ourselves and of our own nature intelligently and according to the facts which are in it, is the best correction for all that slumbering materialism which is concealed even at the heart of our most spiritual conceptions. You remember the

prayer of the prophet Elisha for his servant,—
"Lord, open thou his eyes that he may see."
And the Lord opened the eyes of the young man,
and he saw. He saw a world of beings other
than this, but not far away from it. Our Lord
took his three most ample-minded disciples on to
the Mount of Transfiguration, and their eyes were
opened in a similar way, and they saw — still
embodied, still in recognizable human forms —
Moses and Elias; and they were talking with
Jesus. "The popular notion that before an embodied spirit can be seen it must assume our
material nature, so far at least as to reflect the
light of this world, is exactly the reverse of the
truth; which is that the change must be made in
ourselves; *i.e.*, by opening our spiritual sight." That
which we call "spiritualism," and to which so many
have turned their attention, is the outcry of a bereft
humanity for some knowledge of the departed. And
it would not be wonderful if every now and again
some souls should have their eyes opened and
actually see into the spiritual world. But that is
altogether another thing from that materialization
which Spiritualists announce as possible. There
are no backward movements in Providence. The
grub becomes a butterfly, but the butterfly never
returns to its grub state. Men once emancipated

never return (except by some fiat of Divine Power, as in the case of Lazarus) to material imprisonment. The words of David concerning his departed child, "I shall go to him, but he shall not return to me," express the law of human life. Death is progress, advance disimprisonment.

Shelley has an exquisite passage:—

> "Sudden arose
> Ianthe's soul! It stood
> All beautiful in naked purity,
> The perfect semblance of its bodily frame,
> Instinct with inexpressible beauty and grace.
> Each stain of earthliness
> Had passed away; it reassumed
> Its native dignity, and stood
> Immortal amid ruin."

If only we could accept the truths about death and resurrection out of it, as Paul puts them, and take him as our heaven-appointed teacher, instead of diluting and infiltrating his meaning through so many webs of human opinion, the soul of friend, mother, child, would never be associated with the body that is no longer even a material *body*, but only dust — our heart would be with God all the more because our treasure is with him. And when we approached the great transition ourselves, it would not be with shuddering aversion, but rather in the spirit of that old but expressively beautiful ode: —

> "Vital spark of heavenly flame,
> Quit, oh, quit this mortal frame.
> Trembling, hoping, lingering, flying,
> Oh, the pain, the bliss of dying!
> Cease, fond nature — cease thy strife,
> And let me languish into life.
> Hark! they whisper, angels say —
> 'Sister spirit, come away!'
> What is this confounds me quite,
> Steals my senses, stops my sight,
> Drowns my spirit, draws my breath —
> Tell me, my soul, can this be death?
> The world recedes — it disappears —
> Heaven opens on my eyes — my ears
> With sounds seraphic ring.
> Lend, lend your wings. I mount, I fly!
> O grave, where is thy victory —
> O death, where is thy sting?"

VIII.

THE GREAT TRANSITION.

"You preach death as an enemy instead of a friend and liberator." — GEN. GORDON.

"Oh come that day when in this restless heart
  Earth shall resign her part,
  When in the grave with thee my limbs shall rest,
  My soul with thee be blest!
  But stay, presumptous, — CHRIST with thee abides
  In the rock's dreary sides;
  He from the stone will wring celestial dew,
  If but the prisoner's heart be faithful found and true."
CHRISTIAN YEAR.

VIII.

THE GREAT TRANSITION.

1 Cor. xv. 51. — *Behold, I tell you a mystery: we shall not all sleep, but we shall all be changed.*

A MYSTERY is a truth of revelation, withholden for sufficient reasons, until the time is suitable and reasonable for its disclosure. The Apostle has built up his great argument for man's resurrection from death; resurrection in personal form, and with such embodiment as is suited to his new and higher state. As I tried to show in our last discourse, he repudiates the idea of disembodied spirits; he also repudiates the idea of a material corruptible body as being suited to the condition of human life which follows this. St. Paul regards the material as phenomenal, as having, that is, no consistency in itself, as temporary, as in perpetual change and flux.

That which is substantial, continuing, abiding, is immaterial, of the stuff of which the soul, the mind, the spirit, is made. There is a natural body, a body made out of the material, and there is a spiritual body, a body immaterial, far more substantial than the material, which cannot be corrupted and disintegrated, which cannot be disorganized and destroyed, as this body of our humiliation can be. He calls dying going to sleep, because in sleep there is no recognized communication with the outward material world. Besides, they who sleep do well; sleep has in it the idea of re-invigoration, as well as of cessation from toil. It is a word which contains in it these pleasant ideas of restfulness, of cessation from toil, of re-invigoration, and yet of holding on to life, and so it exactly suits the Apostle. For the heathen word "death" he has less and less of use. Sleep! It is much better. The babe asleep in the cradle is a picture of innocence and beauty. The man asleep rests. The invalid so long as he sleeps a natural sleep is in a hopeful condition. And so the Apostle is enamoured of this word "sleep."

But he has something to say to those who, in the light of the expectation that Christ would come to claim his own, and deliver them out of the grasp of the wickedness of this world, were musing on the destiny of those who would then be alive — still in this body of humiliation.

The Apostle had made it so evident that a flesh-and-blood body could not inherit the kingdom of God — that corruption could not inherit incorruption — that the question naturally came to the front: What of those who are alive and remain when the Master, by his re-appearance, finishes up this dispensation?

The words of our text are an answer to that inquiry — more than an answer: they are light-bringing words. And the light is of the nature of that light which precedes the actual sun-rising. It has in it a tenderness and a vigor-infusing energy recognized by every song-bird in springtime. These words contain the light of the early morning of eternity, "We shall not all sleep; but we shall all be changed, changed in a point of time absolutely indivisible." That is the force of the original word.

"In the twinkling of an eye," a reduplication of the idea. At the last trumpet. In the Scriptures, specially in the book of the Revelation of St. John, every great crisis time is represented as accompanied by the blowing of a trumpet. This period is called the last trumpet-blowing. You will remember that among the Jews the trumpet was used on feast days for the assembling of the people. This is one of the great feast days, the day of Christ's re-appearance to his Church, after his long hiding of himself. Observe how, as the Apostle's thought becomes more spiritual, his language becomes more exalted. Let us not debase it by taking off the angelic garb in which he clothes his thought, and putting on it our soiled every-day raiment. There is nothing so stupid as a perverse literalism. If every preacher could be a poet and a prophet in one, there would be a chance to get some adequate interpretation of the more seraphic scriptures.

We must not miss the suggestion made to us in these words of "an extraordinary work of Divine Omnipotence."

Death is the ordinary way of departure hence. But it is not the only possible way. Yet, sometimes it comes in a flash of lightning. A man's monosyllable is cut in two, and the first half uttered in time is completed only by the second half uttered in eternity. So suddenly does death sometimes come. If only a man's heart be right in the sight of God, that to some of us seems desirable. To others not so. A certain liturgy has in it the prayer, "From sudden death, good Lord, deliver us." We all could join in the petition, "From a painful death — a death in which there is much physical agony, good Lord, deliver us. From a death long and protracted, from days upon days of death, good Lord, deliver us." But in the prayer, "From sudden death, good Lord, deliver us," I, for one, cannot unite.

Does it not seem to you that, in this passage, the Apostle holds out the suddenness of the transition as desirable, and even glorious? In a moment, the transition is made! Bishop Jeremy Taylor has a work on "Holy Living," and another on "Holy Dying." The excited revivalist says, "Prepare to die!" Is Bishop Jeremy Taylor's book on "Holy Dying" apostolic? Is the idea which the excited revivalist thunders apostolic? The man who is preparing to live is the man who is best preparing to die. Even among the old prophets the message was not, "Prepare to die," but, "Prepare to meet thy God, O Israel." That is intelligible. Notice how little of lugubriousness there has been in the Apostle's language in this chapter. There is hardly a mournful sound. Resurrection, triumph, victory, — these are the tones from end to end of it. And in our text there is martial music, and the hosts gather, no longer to fight; for them it is the end of the war, it is the last trump. They that have been, to all seeming, asleep, and they who are alive and remain, all gather, and on these last the great transition comes; they are delivered from their mortality, and from the body of humiliation, in a moment, in the twinkling of an eye, by the Omnipotent Power of God. "As the lightning lighteneth out of the east, and shineth even unto the west, so (to them) shall the coming of the Son of Man be."

In Bengel's Gnomon we have this remark upon this "mystery," to which the Apostle refers: "An extraordinary work of Divine Omnipotence. Who, then, can doubt that man, even at death, may be suddenly freed from sin?" In what way Bengel uses the word "sin" there, I do not know. His idea seems to be this: Cannot he who so suddenly changes the bodily organism from the mortal to the immortal, from the corruptible to the incorruptible, cannot he as suddenly change the soul from unclean to clean, from sinful to righteous? Who can answer? All we can say, is, Possibly, probably.

Once I got, from some source or other, an idea into my mind that all universals are blessings. And I remember how in the lap of it there came this thought: Death is universal; therefore death is a blessing. And I had to say, Yes. But some one says: "Now, I will push him into a corner. Is not sin a universal? is it a blessing?" Whenever there is danger of being indicted for heresy by any self-originated positive affirmation, it is wise to put an Apostle in the place, and let him be condemned first, because condemnation with an Apostle must mean vindication. The answer to the question, "Sin is a universal; is it a blessing?" may be more wisely given in the Apostle's words, "God hath concluded all under sin; that he may have mercy upon all." So far as sin means inherited corruption, so far it puts us in this position, that it makes us objects of the Divine pity and compassion. So far as it is personal wilfulness, it calls for rebuke and repentance. Between guilt and corruption a distinction may be made, if we refer guilt to the action of the will or spiritual powers, and corruption to the action of those involuntary powers of the mind, which are analogous to the involuntary powers of the body.

"Sin is the admission and acceptance by the person of anything that is opposed to reason, and conscience, and the law of God."

The sin of Adam was that he rejected God as a guide and portion, and chose himself as a guide and the world as a portion; and this, account for it as we may, his descendants uniformly do. This is man's prerogative, that he has this power. "In that prerogative of man, by which he can either accept or reject the law of his being, he differs wholly from any mere animal. No animal can approximate anything of the kind. We have here, indeed, a fundamental, perhaps the most fundamental, difference between man and the brute." No brute can be either a fool or a fiend. The Scripture idea of man in his present state is that of a being capable of an indefinite progress, either upward or downward, and of choosing which it shall be.

I say, then, in considering the question of man's

sinfulness, we must make an intelligent analysis of sinfulness. So far as it is an inherited tendency, it is of the nature of corruption, and so puts us under the pity, and entitles us to the mercy, of God; so far as it is deliberate wilfulness, it brings us into antagonism with God. Depend upon it, that no man ever yet struggled against an evil of which he was conscious, persistently and perseveringly, but he ultimately succeeded; for God is on his side all the time. And if he seemed to himself never to conquer till death, in the great deliverance it effects, death itself shall prove to him that he has conquered.

Let us remember that a man is never really subdued till his will is subdued. No man is permanently and fixedly evil till he is willingly evil. Many and many and many a man who has fallen and fallen and fallen has yet never deliberately willed to fall. The best part of his nature has protested all the time. And every man is that which is best in him. Never judge a man by his worst. Always judge him by his best. No single action ever tells you what a man is; only the tendency of his life can tell that. And only God Almighty can fully know it. Therefore let us not judge one another severely,—as much as possible not at all. God hath committed all judgment to his Son because he, and he only, knows us through and through. If we would know what the Apostle means by the words, "He hath concluded all under sin that he may have mercy upon all," it is necessary that we should recognize that sinfulness has this duality in it: it is partly the inherited corruption of the nature and partly wilfulness. For the former we are not responsible; only for the latter. We never know what that great change which comes in death shall do for any character. Even at and in death many and many a man may find that his crowning mercy has come, and that he is suddenly freed from sin.

Anyway, we cannot doubt that the Apostle looks upon this great change of which he speaks as one of the choicest of blessings. The language he uses is the language of exultation. Now, if only we can get a soul within the ribs of death, why, then, death becomes something else than it would otherwise be. It is nonsense to affirm that it does not signify what a man's ideas are, providing his life is right. A man's life is made up of ideas wrought out into practice. Is it not altogether thoughtless, indeed absurd, to say that death to the materialist and to St. Paul means the same? The materialist looks upon death as calamity, as disorganization, as extinction. St. Paul looks upon it as transition; as a dark cloud with a silver lining; as containing a glorious change and a magnificent secret; as a portal to a palace; as the act of introduction to his chiefest and best Friend. And this is why he never feared it. Again and again he went up to it, nor shrank, nor blenched, nor was dismayed.

"To stay here is necessary for the work, but to depart and be with Christ is far better." How absurd to assume that to St. Paul and to the materialist death was the same event! The idea of it each held was totally different, and therefore the feeling each had, when thinking of it, was as darkness is to light. And our happiness and misery in life — are they not made up of thoughts and feelings? Most assuredly. If only we can get light into our ideas and love into our feelings, chronic misery becomes impossible — only possible when we have dark ideas and loveless feelings. Very much less than we think does our happiness depend upon what is external to us. If there be no heaven within, all the externalities of an outward heaven would be insufficient to produce happiness.

Hence, the more you think of it, the more will the teaching of St. Paul appear truth and wisdom. "We shall all be changed." With what exultation he utters those words! Everywhere the New Testament speaks of change; "regeneration" is the word often used, but it is the same idea. Have you never been wearied by the thought of life, as it is now, continuing on and on? Supposing Immortality should be the perpetuation of our life *just as it is;* are there not times when you doubt whether it would be a benediction? Do not men speak of the weary burden of life? Yes, indeed. The Apostle comes to our rescue, and adds his simple words, "We shall all be changed." Then, what hopes, what anticipations, what possibilities! "We shall all be changed!" "Corruption shall put on incorruption; the mortal shall put on Immortality." "We shall all be changed." Death shall be swallowed up of victory; death, of which disease is but the forerunner, the reminder, the precursor, having a constant taste of death in it; so that the perpetually diseased are perpetually sipping at Death's bitter cup. But "we shall all be changed." That day we spent on our Mount of Transfiguration, when we said to our Lord, "It is good for us to be here; let us make here a permanent abiding-place"; that day was a promise of what is coming. It was a bird of paradise let loose from its confines to sing its song for awhile, and then disappear. For like as a man is to be judged by his best, so life is to be judged by what it has been in its best moments.

The best is always the truest. The best is always that which is nearest heaven. The best is always that likest God. Recall your best days, recall your gladdest hours, recall your seasons when the heart was purest, and when tears ran down your cheeks, not because you were sad, but because you were glad, for in that direction the change has to come. Oh, you don't know yet what Christianity is. You have seen it in poverty, in want, in weakness, in woe. A poor wayfaring man, struggling with his hard fate, kicked, buffeted, despised, persecuted, jeered at by badly trained children, dogs let loose upon him — even as such an one has Christianity been in the world, — a candle in a dark room, a light in a dark place, a sweet song amid discords, a heavenly toned voice drowned in Babel sounds; but its day is coming. The heavenly toned voice will rise above and still the Babel sounds; the sweet song will penetrate and harmonize the discords; the light will illumine the dark place till all the darkness flies; the candle will increase in brightness till it becomes a sun; the poor despised man will rise up in the dignity of a king, — "King of Kings and Lord of Lords."

IX.

THE STING OF DEATH.

"The doctrine of hereditary corruption is so far from being contradictory to modern ideas, that it may be said to be a direct corollary from the doctrine of evolution." — PRINCIPAL TULLOCH.

"Sin can have no tenure by law at all, but is rather an eternal outlaw, and in hostility with law past all atonement; both diagonal contraries, as much allowing one another as day and night together in one hemisphere." — MILTON.

"Guilt, though it may attain temporal splendor, can never confer real happiness." — SIR WALTER SCOTT.

IX.

THE STING OF DEATH.

1 COR. xv. 56. — *The sting of death is sin; and the power of sin is the law, but thanks be unto God which giveth us the victory, through our Lord Jesus Christ.*

THE words between the fifty-second and the fifty-sixth verses of this chapter are an amplification of the thought on which we have already dwelt. In this passage there is a new idea, — a reminder of what it is in death which hurts. That the Apostle should speak of death as a venomous beast is natural. He is thinking of the Garden of Eden and its serpent. Therefore, he refers to the "sting" of death. Sin is that sting. Sin! what is it? The word has come to be so theological that it has almost been lifted out of the region of our ordinary thought and speech. It hardly stands as a synonym for the words "wrong," "wickedness," "crime." And yet it means that which is denoted by these words, and more. It goes deeper than these words go. It suggests a wilful, depraved, and corrupt *state*, not simply wicked and corrupt deeds and acts, but a biassed, inward condition. Apart from his deeds, man is sinful. Suppose there could be a case of a man who had never consciously done any corrupt act; still the effort which such a man had made to abstain from bad deeds, — the fight he had had with himself, — would indicate an inward depravity. So that the Scripture representation, — "There is none righteous; no, not one"; "God hath concluded all under sin, that he may have mercy upon all," — suggests a rule without any exception. In this condition it is very unbecoming in us to reproach each other with depravity. The same nature is in us all, and that nature has in it everywhere a corruptedness inherited from the past. Can we get any intelligent idea of that corruptedness? Can we understand it? How came it? The question will in our day be answered by men of different schools of thought according to their views of human nature. After examining all the views which have been presented, I am persuaded that the New-Testament view of the case is the most satisfactory, because it goes to the root of the matter, and not simply because it is that of Jesus of Nazareth and his disciples. Your patience with me would be gone long before I had arrived at the end of the theme, if I reviewed the various theories which have been advanced on the question of what sin is, and how it came into our nature. I propose no such use or waste of your time. I may be excused, however, if

I make a very brief reference to the view of sin which is held by the most recent school of scientific investigators and by the spiritual minds in that school. The evolutionists undertake to account for human depravity in this way: Man's bodily organism has been evolved from the lower animal organisms. In it there remains a tendency towards a reversion to the original type. That is one of the discovered laws in nature. Our domesticated creatures all exhibit that tendency. Not only so: flowers manifest it; the choicest floral results depend on cultivation. The exquisitely beautiful tints and tones of color in flowers have been developed under the care of man. Cease caring for these flowers, and every one of them tends to revert to its former type. So with animals, — dogs and horses: under man's influence they have become the noble and useful creatures they are; but that influence and training have to be continued or these creatures will revert to their former wild and savage condition. Man has, in his physical organism, — say the more open-minded men of this school, — reminiscences of his animal origin. While he has in him something found in no animal, — that which apprehends the invisible and eternal, — he has also that which is merely animal. "Hence it is that the flesh lusteth against the Spirit, and the Spirit against the flesh." In a very few words, and, of course, very inadequately, — but with sufficient lucidity for our purpose, — that represents the most recent view of human depravity from the scientific side of things. There is nothing in it unreasonable or unintelligent, — nothing which is in violent antagonism to anything which has been taught us by the Apostle Paul. So orthodox a man as President McCosh accepts it as a statement not at all anti-biblical. But while there is nothing in that statement of the case very objectionable, yet it does not seem altogether sufficient. It throws the odium of our sinful capability back on him who made us, and says, "Why hast thou made me thus?" That feeling which the poet of Scotland put into such charming verse, when death was staring him in the face, has, I doubt not, often been in ourselves : —

"O Thou, unknown, almighty Cause
   Of all my hope and fear,
In whose dread presence ere an hour
   Perhaps I must appear,

"If I have wandered in those paths
   Of life I ought to shun, —
As something loudly in my breast
   Remonstrates I have done, —

"Thou know'st that Thou hast formed me
   With passions wild and strong;
And listening to their witching voice
   Has often led me wrong."

To some persons this may seem very irreverent. To go into the Divine Presence and say, "I was born so; born with these tendencies, these passions wild and strong"—that seems, doubtless, to some, almost unpardonable audacity. But why should Burns be condemned, and David excused? "Behold I was shapen in iniquity, and in sin did my mother conceive me." What is that but saying to the Almighty, "I did not originate these tendencies; I inherited them." The deep reverence of the soul is in itself a most excellent endowment. Is that reverence inconsistent with the utmost honesty in the expression of feeling and conviction? We know how difficult it is to be perfectly candid in the presence of each other. Oftentimes that want of candor proceeds from a good feeling; the fear of offending or wounding another; or the fear of misleading. Minds are in different degrees of advance, and that which would be understood by minds in one stage of growth would be misunderstood in another and earlier stage.

Into the Divine Presence we can go with the most perfect candor. Our God knows us, and he knows us altogether. Omniscience thus becomes a harbor of refuge for us. And there is no religious exercise of the soul more salutary than that in which we go into the closet and shut the door and pour out everything before God. The soul seems to get cleansed by it, and be set to new resolves in a new strength.

And this perfect candor — does it not mean perfect confidence? What is it that keeps even the nearest friends from a thorough unbosomment of themselves to one another? Is it not lack of confidence? Now, when a man goes into the Divine Presence, in an act of private devotion, and empties his doubts and fears and suspicions and apprehensions on that Unseen Altar by which the High Priest of humanity perpetually stands, does he not honor his Lord by his confidence? "I can tell Thee all, O my God, and believe still that Thou wilt not despise me!" Now where there is perfect confidence there is no irreverence. The one great, grand, glorious, wonderful thing in true motherhood is its readiness to forgive all and everything to the prodigal son, and take him back again into the arms of love, in the belief that there is something worth saving. I can never think of the tremendous obstinacy which there is in a mother's affection for her son, without wondering. And yet, is it not the best thing there is on this earth of ours? The way in which a mother will perversely believe that her son is this, that, and the other, when everybody else sees that he is not — the way in which she will yield to him, and coax him, and flatter him, and make him believe in himself as something vastly superior to the ordinary run of folks — is there anything on earth so deliciously obstinate, and beautiful, and ridiculous? And yet is there anything on earth so near heaven? The scientific Calvinist comes along and says: "That is weakness. It is a sign of human depravity." Then I say, thank God for human depravity if it is capable of such loving perversity of blind belief in a good under all the evil. Now, as a son can go with all his wrecked life into the presence of that mother, and she will believe in him still, and will even be thankful for his confidence in her, so I believe, on the testimony of all the highest teaching in Scripture, that a sinning soul can go with the utmost candor into the Divine Presence, and not be thrust out, not be denied audience. The good feeling which follows such unbosoming is an evidence of the acceptance a soul gets even when it goes like David and says, "Behold, I was shapen in iniquity," or like Burns, —

> "Thou knowest Thou hast formed me
> With passions wild and strong;
> And listening to their witching voice
> Has often led me wrong."

This poet found, when in the very presence of death, that the sting of death is sin. A sinful consciousness accompanies us all through life. It darkens everything. Specially does it hang a heavy cloud over the fact we call death; a cloud different in density and darkness to different men, according to the life they have lived. To some it is black, very black. To others it is a cloud through which the sun of righteousness shines, brilliant with purple and gold, betokening a fine to-morrow.

The Apostle's second thought is the relation of sin to law. I am afraid that any discussion of this relation would seem to you very dry and uninteresting. But if you will have patience with me for only a minute or two, I will try to suggest what the Apostle means by these words, "The strength (or power) of sin is the law." He does not mean Jewish law simply or chiefly, but moral law. That moral law is only a part of that great moral order which is behind all moral life. St. Paul taught that "man is a moral being subject to Divine authority,"—in other words, a subject of law. He takes man, and, placing him before the mirror of divine law, shows him all the ruin and sadness of his moral state. The more man knew of the divine law of righteousness, the more incompetent, incapable, and sinful he appeared. Physically, mentally, and spiritually he was a sinner. He had not kept the law of righteousness. Most men had not even tried to keep it. They had scoffed at it, and treated it with contempt and disdain. When death came near, and conscience began to accuse, this despised law written in the nature, written on the heart, written on the two tables of stone, began to force itself into recognition, and the more men had consciously broken it, the more terrible death was to them. Thus the law used by the conscience became the power of sin. The law did not create sin. It only revealed its sinfulness. How? In this way: When by the side of a crooked line you draw a straight one, how the crookedness of the crooked line appears! When by the side of an inferior painting you put a finished artist's work, how the inferiority of the one is emphasized! In the same way all excellency makes inferiority appear what it is. Unrighteousness has an excuse for itself until righteousness is put alongside it. When the moral law of God was issued, how sinful the life of the Jewish people appeared, — how depraved that heathen life all around them! And so says the Apostle, "by the law was the knowledge of sin." Not sin, but the knowledge of it. The conscience took the law of God and made it live in the soul of the dying man; and thus the sense of sin was aggravated by the existence of the law with its unrelenting frown. That, in brief, is what the Apostle means when he says "the power of sin is the law."

But he does not stop at that. Pictured before his

mind is One who comes to rescue man from the lashings of conscience — from the thunderings of law. In the very language which the Apostle uses, a vivid but sanctified imagination is at work. He sees a man battling with his own conscience, and battling with law; he sees a man in presence of Mount Sinai, when the moral law of God was given and there were lightnings and thunderings; he sees a man wrapped in the folds of the angry tempest, cowed, conscience-stricken, terrified. Then he sees another, stronger and mightier than he, haste to his rescue, and, delivering him from the angry storm and blinding tempest, take him to a place of refuge, soothe him and care for him, speaking peace to his perturbed soul, and thus awakening love in his fluttering heart. Then the Apostle breaks out into jubilant praise, "But thanks be to God which giveth us the victory, through our Lord Jesus Christ." This is the crowning thought; this is the consummation of the life that begins in ignorance — a mere seed sown — developed through the discipline of suffering and trial, yielding to sin, sorrowing for sin, battling with sin, eventually seized upon by death — a life which on the outside seems so much of a mystery; a problem so insoluble; an existence for which there is no adequate cause or reason; a struggle and a defeat. That is how it looks on the outside; but when we get to the inside of it, as by the help of this Apostle we do in this chapter, the darkness is shot through with light; the problem begins to be workable; the mystery begins to write itself in language that we can decipher. Sin is not everything; punishment is not everything; the flesh is not everything; this mortal body is not everything; law is not supreme; conscience is not supreme. For in the very act of dying, when defeat seems certain and inevitable, — when the man can no longer hold out against the forces that threaten him, — when his own strength seems entirely and finally failing, — then it is that the Apostle shouts his pæan of victory, "Thanks be unto God who giveth us the victory, through our Lord Jesus Christ."

Let us not miss a word in this passage. It is victory not won, but given. It is victory not earned, not deserved, not accomplished, but given. Sin is in the man. Conscience is lashing him. Death's maw is open to receive him. He is in extremity. He can do nothing. He can fight no longer. The struggle is over. He has no power left. It is then, *then*, — EVEN THEN, — in the very hour of seeming defeat, that the exulting voice is heard, "Thanks be unto God who giveth us the victory, through our Lord Jesus Christ."

Now, if the victory comes through our Lord Jesus Christ, through his relation to us and our relation to him, what in the world have we to do with any form or kind of theologic teaching which does not make of Jesus Christ all that the New Testament makes of him? Sin is a fact, death is a fact, conscience is a fact, law is a fact. In all these facts, work them together how you will, there is no gospel. One man says to me, "Be conscientious." There is no gospel in that. Another says, "Comply with the moral law — be moral." There is no gospel in that. Another reminds me that I am a sinner, and that I must die. There is no gospel in that. Turn about these thoughts as you will, in any order you will; keep travelling within the area of these four facts — sin, death, conscience, law; keep inside them; do not get outside them — there is no gospel in that area. Never until we add, "victory, through our Lord Jesus Christ," do we find the storm abating, the winds lulled into peace, the thunders moderating their tone till they become zephyrs, whispering quiet into the soul; never till we add, "victory, through our Lord Jesus Christ," does the conscience approve; never till then does the law of life become the law of love.

X.

CERTAIN REWARD.

" If materialism is the scourge of society, religion is its saviour; if the one desolates the heart, the other soothes and strengthens it." — LOUIS FIGUIER.

" I would cut off my own head if it had nothing better in it but wit; and tear out my own heart if had no better disposition than to love only myself and laugh at all my neighbors." — POPE.

" Let us do good without hope of recompense; let us fulfil our duty without ostentation; and our name will live among people of worth." — FREDERICK THE GREAT.

X.

CERTAIN REWARD.

1 Cor. xv. 58. — Wherefore, my beloved brethren, be ye steadfast, unmoveable, always abounding in the work of the Lord, forasmuch as ye know that your labor is not vain in the Lord.

THE first word of this passage is a connective: "Wherefore" — taking these facts and truths — these reasonings and arguings from the relations which have come to us in Christ Jesus our Lord,—"wherefore, my beloved brethren, be ye steadfast, unmoveable, always abounding in the work of the Lord, forasmuch as ye know that your labor is not vain in the Lord." This is the practical application of the whole truth of this fifteenth chapter, the practical application so far as it can be brought within the conditions of time and space.

The Christian disciple is in the world; he is not taken hence as soon as his discipleship begins. He is left here with a new and higher relationship to the world in which he lives. Every new truth means a new work. No truth is given to a man to be hoarded by him. Everything is for support and for use. One reason, I verily believe, why many are always learning and never coming to a knowledge of the truth, is, that they have no set intent and purpose to use truth, to employ it, to make it practical and operative. They want it for comfort simply. They want it for a bed to lie on; for a pillow on which to recline a somnolent brain; not to enlighten and direct them along the road of duty and benevolence. Does it not seem to us improbable that the spirit of God would ever give men light simply for speculative and controversial purposes? If we do not need God's truth for the legitimate purposes of our everyday life, is it not best that we should be without it? Moreover, the use of a truth seems to be necessary to our really knowing it. The condition of knowing what the teaching of Christ is seems to be willingness to do the Divine Will. "He that doeth the will shall know of the teaching, whether it be of God."

There are three leading ideas in this text of ours, and they may be indicated by the three words, Restfulness, Activity, Confidence. As we read this utterance of the Apostle's, it brings to our memory the old words, "In returning and rest shall ye be saved; in quietness and confidence shall be your strength." In every life there needs to be a restful centre if there is to be a wise and well-ordered activity. The ocean itself could not bring back into quiet and order its foaming waves, lashed into anger by the roaring hurricane, if it had not a deep peace underneath — a peace never disturbed by the loudest and most turbulent tempest. I know of nothing in our own day more painfully and surely indicative of the interior wrongness of our life than the inability everywhere manifest to rest and be quiet. No life was ever healthy and strong in which there was not a central rest, and something to feed and support that rest. But in our day the question "what shall I do next?" is asked before we have well finished that which went before. And so, much of our activity is blind and purposeless. It is merely wasting and consuming time. There is no virtue in it, and no intelligence in it; consequently no profit. Life does not become purified, or strengthened, or enriched, or made happier thereby. It is simply squandered. Now, all this is not simply wrong; it is foolish. It is not simply harmless activity; it is the activity that comes from internal hollowness of nature. We congratulate ourselves on being the most "alive" people in the world — which means in plain English, the most restless. But mere restlessness has no inherent virtue or goodness in it. It simply denotes the possession of vitality, which vitality may be altogether uneducated and untrained.

In every useful life there must be internal rest. There must be something believed in so firmly and so continuously that it holds to itself the mind and heart. Therefore it is that the Apostle says, "Be ye steadfast, unmoveable." Consider who it is gives utterance to these words. It is the man of all others most intensely active, the Apostle who was here, there, and everywhere in the Roman world. But his activity was all of a piece. It was animated by a single purpose, — that of making known to men the truth that had come to us in Christ Jesus. In that he rested. He was steadfast and immovable in regard to that. This man had no doubts that Jesus was the Messiah, the unique Son of God, the Redeemer of Man, God's great light sent into the world. You cannot find in all Paul's writings any evidence of unsettledness on the character and claims of Jesus of Nazareth. Steadfastly and immovably he was fixed to that centre. Everywhere in his letters he assumes that man is so made constitutionally that this Jesus Christ is pre-adapted to him.

When the Eternal Father gave us Jesus Christ, he gave us one who is pre-harmonized to our necessities. When the heart rests in him, it rests finally. When the mind rests in him, it rests as the astronomer rests who has found his sun. When once Copernicus got the sun at the centre, it forever remained there. Though the prejudice and bigotry of his day said he was wrong, he knew that he was right. In our day nothing needs to be uttered more dogmatically and with more earnestness than this: that for every heart and mind there must be a centre of affection; a centre of light to which we can look, always and ever, without doubt and fear, without vacillation and variableness. Does it seem to you possible that there should be in us the necessity for some One who can be to us a resting-place for mind and heart, and no one to meet that necessity? Wherever you find hunger, you find food; wherever you find intelligence, you find objects which appeal to it; wherever you find the sense of beauty, you find scenes that are lovely and beautiful to meet and feed and gratify that sense — and so of all other senses and faculties. Every sense has its food suited to it. In our nature there is a craving for some steadfast and abiding centre of life on which we can rest, towards which we can turn and say, "That centre remains the centre; that abides; I can fix my mind on it; I can fix my heart on it." God knows we need such a centre. Our nature has developed the need. The Romanist system supplies an infallible Pope. That system has grown out of this deep need. It seems to us, however, that infallibility does not belong to any sinful creature, nor to any number of sinful creatures in conclave or council assembled. No prophet or apostle claims infallibility, and yet the infallible centre is needed. We have it in Christ Jesus. According to the apostolic testimony, he is the same yesterday, to-day, and forever. He is God's answer to our need. There is no reason or sense in St. Paul's urging us to be steadfast and unmovable, unless we have a steadfast and unmovable centre on which to rest our affection and trust.

The more I think about it, the deeper is my persuasion that, in these days of ours, it is more than unwise to put anything on the level of the authority which, in the constitution of things, Christ has over the human soul. Creeds have their place and their use, but they are human compilations. They are liable to err in putting the emphasis on the wrong word, and also in stating in the fixed and unelastic language of man that which belongs to the luminous and eternal thought of God. All commentaries, sermons, expositions, are man's fallible work. They stand or fall like anything else of man's. At best they are helps — never of the nature of authority that may not be disputed or questioned. There is but one Lord — Jesus the Christ; one faith — faith in him; one baptism — the baptism of the Holy Spirit; one God and Father of all, who is above all, and through all, and in you all. We do not lack infallibility. In all things where infallibility is possible and essential we have it in our Jesus, God's Christ. This explains why the Apostle Paul was so tremendously dogmatic in some things, and so accommodating in others. In this very epistle he says, "If any man loveth not the Lord, let him be Anathema."

And yet, in another place he says, "To the Jews I became as a Jew, that I might gain the Jews; to them that are without law as without law, — I became all things to all men, if by any means I might save some." What are we to make of this man? How do you explain this doubleness? Only on the principle that the facts about Jesus the Christ, his relation to God and man, are of another kind and order from any human arrangements, or opinions, or interpretations. There is nothing that has dishonored Christ more than the elevating of matters of opinion to the level of dogmatic Christian truth. It has produced schism upon schism. It has divided the Church. It has mystified the minds of men. It has developed the worst types of the irreligious spirit. It has made infidels by hundreds and thousands. There is One, and One only, who, because of his elevation in nature, in purpose, in work, in achievement, is the Infallible Centre of a Christian's trust and hope. Concerning him and the facts of his life, "Be ye steadfast, *steadfast;* YES, SO STEAD-FAST that ye are positively and absolutely immovable." In him rest.

When you have attained to that rest, then your activity will have a limit, a direction, and an aim. The area within which you can exercise yourself is large enough for the employment of all your faculties. What heartiness there is in these words, "Always abounding in the work of the Lord!" How you feel the man of Tarsus in them! As to time, we are to do the work of the Lord always. As to quantity, we are to abound in it. As to the kind of work, it is to be the work of the Lord. There is room enough here for every one who has the true Christian spirit. There is room for every kind of work that a man can do, feeling, while he is doing it, "I can ask God's blessing on my work."

We must not limit the work of the Lord to that which is strictly ecclesiastical. Everything which does good to the bodies, minds, souls of men is the work of the Lord. We are in God's world. As disciples of Christ, we have rights here which are indisputable. In the light of the truth which the Apostle brings before us in this chapter, we can discern that everything which recognizes man as moving onward towards the realization of a nobler inward and outward condition than that to which he has already attained, is work of the Lord. In the light of the truth which fills this chapter, and considering that it is addressed to Christian disciples, we may infer that the tendency of this truth of man's escape through death into life is to promote activity in the work of the Lord. Yea, I am persuaded that if we could only get the truth of this great argument into our souls, it would give us such rest of heart and such energy of life, that we should know how necessary rest of heart is to labor, and see that the willing activity of hopeful, vigorous Christians is the sign and proof of the deep peace they have within. There are in the Church of Christ those who, by reason of physical decrepitude, have ever to remind themselves of Milton's splendid line, "They also serve who only stand and wait." But does it not seem to you that some form of Christian service is sure to follow a vigorous inward faith? Oh, I wish it were possible to believe that there are no men and women, of a Christianized sort, who are ever seeking for types of religion which, without rebuke, will allow them to spend far more time and money in providing trivial and foolish entertainments for themselves than they ever spend in the work of the Lord. It was in view of this class of persons, — persons who even ask, "How near may I go to being everything, and doing everything that a respectable non-Christian person does, and yet not lose my Christianity altogether?" — in view of this class of persons, that Dr. John Henry Newman uttered that celebrated sentence: "I will not shrink from uttering my firm conviction that it would be a gain to this country were it vastly more superstitious, more bigoted, more gloomy, more fierce in its religion than at present it shows itself to be. Not, of course, that I think the tempers of mind herein implied desirable, which would be an evident absurdity, but I think them infinitely more desirable and more promising than a heathen obduracy, and a cold, self-sufficient, self-wise indifference." Of course, in order to do the work of the Lord, a man must believe in the Lord with a different kind of belief from that which merely assents, in the sense of not caring to dispute the matter. He must believe, also, in the view of man's nature, and of what is before it, which the Apostle gives us in this chapter. A man who cannot stand upright cannot, of course, walk — much less, run. And a man whose faith has no backbone in it can do nothing but crawl, or float about, to and fro, like a jelly-fish with the advancing and receding tide. If a church is to abound in the work of the Lord, it must be a church of men and women (yes; and children, for I dare not think of them as outsiders) who are mentally and affectionally alive. Such a church needs to be fed with "strong meat" for men, as well as with "milk" for babes. A healthy man, full of life, has a good appetite for strong food. That will give him exuberance of life. Activity he must have; he must work at something. So is it mentally: fill a man's mind with truth, — such truth as has come to us in Jesus Christ, such truth as St. Paul has put into this chapter, — and the receiver of that truth will want to incorporate it in some way. No truth is adequately apprehended until it creates inward energy. Truth acts on the mind precisely as material food acts on the body. It either creates warmth and energy, or it creates indigestion. I think that there can be no doubt that good, solid Biblical truth, — such as Jesus taught, such as Paul preached, — does not agree with some constitutions. There is such a condition as that of mental and spiritual indigestion. In that case the food is not at fault, but the digestion is impaired. Let man, woman, or child try to satisfy the cravings of appetite on candies and ice-creams — what then? The digestive apparatus will become so impaired that it cannot assimilate the nutritive elements in solid food — so is it mentally; so is it spiritually. There are whole congregations of men and women to be found who cannot assimilate Scripture truth. Their mental digestion has been ruined by the ice-cream of Rationalism, and the luscious confections of an emotional and superstitious form of religion. St. Paul's "strong meat" they cannot digest. But to those who can digest it, what nutriment there is in it! — what inward warmth it creates! what energy it generates! what varied activities ensue! — so that of such it may be said, "They are always abounding in the work of the Lord."

The third thought suggested by the Apostle's words is that of confidence: "Forasmuch as ye know that your labor is not vain in the Lord." Every one engaged in any department of the vineyard of the Lord needs, at some time or other, just these words. The Apostle himself had been seemingly defeated again and again. Yet he was always confident. It seems to me that he intended, in these words, to suggest to the mind of all Christian workers the idea that to work for the kingdom of God was certain to be profitable with some kind of profit. A man working along the lines of a true Christian effort could never work in vain. Even when we seem to be unsuccessful, — even when we seem to be defeated, — we are not working in vain. Has it never occurred to you that there was a divine mercifulness in what has been sometimes phrased the "non-success" of our Lord's ministry? At the end of his earthly life there was nothing to show but a small band of followers — all but all of them poor, working men. The end of his earth-life seemed defeat, — and defeat of the most odious kind. Nothing for him but the Cross. Yet that defeat, as we now see it, was the most splendid victory. Christianity would lack its most pathetic element if the Cross were not in it. It would lack that revelation which most tenderly appeals to the heart of man. And there are hundreds of men who, in doing the work of the Lord, have seemed to be defeated. In doing it, they have had to bear a heavy cross. I believe that when that light of Eternity, which shall search men and movements to their centre, shall be poured around the deeds of men, there will be revelations, not a few, showing that seeming defeat has, in the judgment of the Master, been victory. "He who never breaks the bruised reed," he who "never quenches the smoking flax," will show that the work about which we have been most discouraged has not been "vain in the Lord." Anyway, I prefer to credit the great Apostle when he affirms, "Forasmuch as ye know that your labor is not vain in the Lord." With the New Testament in my hand, I cannot believe in some of our methods of estimating the value of church work. Arithmetical figures can never express spiritual results. The hysteric efforts to make "a good showing" before the world, or even before the churches, are not endorsed by anything that I can find in the New Testament. There is a commercial side to church life which needs consecrated commercial faculty to perform it. But we cannot introduce the spirit of ecclesiastical competition into our church life without lowering our spiritual tone. When any of us work for the approval and applause of men, rather than out of a feeling of service to God, we shall have our reward, but it will never satisfy us; steadily it will disappoint us, and eventually we shall give up our work.

But if, seeing the excellency of Christian work as well as its necessity, we are willing to take our place, any place that seems to need us, we act in the spirit of that saintly soul who sang : —

> "Dismiss me not thy service, Lord,
> But train me to thy will;
> For even I, in fields so broad,
> Some duty may fulfil;
> And I will ask for no reward
> Except to serve thee still."

If in that spirit we take our place, choose our work, and do it, then we have a right to believe that our labor shall not be in vain in the Lord. God will be glorified; into ourselves there will come a character which shall adapt us to the next stage of life, and other souls will inevitably be impressed and influenced. Our feelings mislead us. Our views of God's work and of our own nature are short-sighted. Let us trust the divine word that has come to us through one of the noblest men who ever lived. Remembering the greatest of historical facts so abundantly attested by so many witnesses — remembering that there is no sufficient reason for Paul's heroic life, except that he gives himself; that the risen Lord met and called him into apostleship — remembering that our Lord's own life is the root out of which all other consecrated Christian lives have grown — remembering that in his keeping are they who have fallen asleep; that they have a conscious personal existence still — remembering that our Lord is exalted to put down all rule and all authority and power that is antagonistic to man's welfare — remembering that this life of ours is only a life introductory and preliminary to the true and full human life, which God designed for us, when he said, "Let us make man in our image, after our likeness" — remembering that flesh and blood cannot inherit the Kingdom of God; that there is first a natural body suited to earth, and then a spiritual body suited to the Paradise beyond — remembering that as we have borne the image of the earthy, we shall also bear the image of the heavenly; that this corruption must put on incorruption, and this mortal must put on Immortality; — remembering all this, then death has lost its sting; the grave has lost its victory. Death is the portal to sinlessness, to the glad, free health of Paradise, to nobler mental and spiritual conditions. Remembering that it is not a continuation simply of this poor, stained, feeble life we are promised, but that we shall all be changed — remembering also that this eternal life is not something earned, or something deserved, or something won, but that the victory is given through our Lord Jesus Christ; — remembering these great and glorious facts and truths, "Wherefore, my beloved brethren, be ye steadfast, unmoveable, always abounding in the work of the Lord, forasmuch as ye know that your labor is not vain in the Lord."

I have now travelled with you along the route which the Apostle has macadamized to our tread. My aim was to try to enrich your Christain thought and illumine your Christian hope. I have consulted everything I could lay my hands on to verify the meaning of every important word in every sentence. I have given you only the results, never the processes. More and more I look upon the Christian minister as an interpreter. His business is to get, by processes sometimes laborious and long-continued, at the exact meaning of the Scriptures, and preach that which he finds there. Consequently, a minister who is faithful to the Scriptures can never preach simply as a denominationalist. The moment a pulpit becomes denominational in its teaching, it necessarily becomes partial and defective. It cannot be honestly scriptural. May God grant that by the help of the truth which this great servant of God has brought to us, we may be able to look forward even hopefully to that great change which shall separate us from our present limited and depraved conditions, and introduce us into a purer, freer, nobler, larger life, where the light and love of God shall lift the soul into a beatitude which shall be an Eternal Te Deum : —

"THANKS BE UNTO GOD WHICH GIVETH US THE VICTORY, THROUGH OUR LORD JESUS CHRIST."

www.ingramcontent.com/pod-product-compliance
Lightning Source LLC
Chambersburg PA
CBHW030249170426
43202CB00009B/679